How ... Heaven

The easy way

Ray Westbrook

How to Get to Heaven the Easy Way
By Ray Westbrook
Published by **Westbrook Publishing**
http://www.HowToGetToHeaven.org

How to Get to Heaven 3

Introduction

My goal in writing this book is to present the truths of God as written in His Holy Bible which will determine where you will spend eternity.

This is a commonsense look at the Bible and God's plan for mankind. I have been studying the Bible for several decades. However, wisdom does not come necessarily with knowing facts or obtaining college degrees. Wisdom is one of the subjects of this book and we will learn that it comes from a higher source, from God Himself.

I believe that the Bible is the inerrant Word of God, period. I believe that if you are sincerely open, not only within your brain for learning but also within your heart for wisdom, the truths in this book can change where you will spend eternity. This is a guidebook for **how to get to heaven**.

This will occur not from any knowledge or wisdom I have to impart, but from the Almighty God of creation opening your heart and mind to the truth. Many hundreds of millions of people over the centuries have been "saved" and are on their way to heaven because of the timeless truths set forth in the Word of God.

Acknowledgments

I would like to thank the people in my life, who at various times have led me from the wrong path, the one that leads to eternal destruction to the right path, an eternity with God.

First and foremost, the Lord Jesus Christ, for saving me from eternal separation from God the Father.

John Yoak a brother that had a major influence in my initial walk with God. Pastor Chuck Smith, Calvary Chapel; Chuck Missler, Koinonia House; Pastor Bob Nash, Chapel of the Cascades; Pastor Geoff Nelson, Cornerstone Fellowship; and Jerry Lenhard, Calvary Chapel, Tri-Counties.

There are many others over the years who, through various means, God has used to enlighten to me to the truths of God.

To all these men and women I will be eternally grateful.

This book could not have happened without the help and support of my lovely wife Sheila.

Chapter 1
Eternity

Where is He Now?

I would like to paint a picture for you. A death has occurred. This person who has just died was a very rich and influential man. He was financially well off, a billionaire. He was a statesman, loved by all, a great humanitarian. He did enormous good in his life. He owned five mansions throughout the world. He had acquired hundreds of beautiful art pieces and donated them to museums. His wife and children loved him. This man would be remembered as a great man and rightfully so. He, no doubt, would be in the history books. He had accomplished great things in his life.

Do you have a good picture of this person? He was a person who was greater than most of us. But as you are in the funeral home looking down at this man in his magnificent coffin, the question occurs to you, "where is this man now?" Right now, this very moment? For this particular man, at this particular moment, this is the only thing that matters now. You suddenly realize he did not take anything with him. All of his wealth, power, prestige, worldly possessions, all that he owned does not really matter to him now.

The only thing that really matters at this point is where is this man now? As the Bible says: "life is very short, like a vapor."

James 4:14
Whereas you do not know what will happen tomorrow. For what is your life? It is even a vapor that appears for a little time and then vanishes away.

How Long is Eternity?

Eternity on the other hand is forever, a very, very long time. So it stands to reason that all a person does in this life, all that he accomplishes, all that he learns, all the decisions he makes, should be subordinate to the preparation for eternity. Wouldn't you agree?

In reality, for the man in this scenario and for most people on the earth today, this is the area to which the least amount of time and effort is devoted. They will spend years, even decades obtaining degrees, learning a trade, or a job, but very little time, if any, preparing for eternity. Seems kind of dumb and irresponsible when put like that, doesn't it?

You never know how much time you have left on this earth. You may be days, hours, or minutes away from stepping off this planet and entering into eternity. No one who dies from an accident or a sudden fatal illness ever thought when leaving the house that morning that he would never return. Accidents and heart attacks are usually sudden and unexpected.

Now that he is lying in the box, you can't help wondering, if he could do it again, where would he put his time and energy? How can we know, for sure, where we are going after death? Stay tuned.

Intellectualism – a Stumbling Block

The above statement is against all that seems to be right. Isn't smarter better? Isn't knowledge the key to all things? Just remember, knowledge and wisdom are not synonymous. Intellectualism and common sense are not equal. You could be the most intellectual person in the world and not be able to put your knowledge to practical use without just plain common sense.

Knowledge is the ability to know about things, accumulating facts. Wisdom is the ability to discern the truth, to have understanding of a matter. The Bible says true wisdom comes from God through His Word, the Bible. This statement is either right or wrong. You will either believe this statement in the Bible or not! The interesting phenomenon about the truth is that it doesn't matter whether you believe it or not, **truth is truth**. Whether you believe it or not doesn't change it.

I can enter your home and tell you someone just ran into your car on the street and that it's wrecked! You may respond, "I don't believe you!" That does not alter the fact that your car is wrecked. It is wrecked whether you believe it or not. So, truth is truth. The best we can hope for is that we can discern the truth from falsehood.

The Bible makes it clear that God, in His revealed Word, has given His message to mankind so that the average person can know God, and can know His plan for mankind. You don't have to be a priest or a minister or an intellectual to understand the Word of God. You don't have to be a genius or even be very smart. The Bible states the opposite. You do, however, have to have a true and genuine desire to know truth, to know God, and what His plan is for man and for your life.

Matthew 11:25
At that time Jesus said, "I praise you, Father, Lord of heaven and earth, because you have hidden these things from the ***wise and learned****, and revealed them* ***to little children."***

The Teaching of Evolution

Did you ever stop to think why it is that most of the philosophers, doctors, scientists, and intellectuals in general, believe we crawled out of the slimy ooze, when the preponderance of evidence points to man being created? These people are considered to be the intellectuals of the world, yet they mislead many. Since God has something to say on this matter, as He does on every subject, let's see what He says:

Romans 1:20-23
For since the creation of the world, God's invisible qualities– his eternal power and divine nature– have been clearly seen, ***being understood from what has been made****, so* ***that men are without excuse****.*
For although they knew God, they neither glorified him as God nor gave thanks to him, but their thinking became futile and their foolish hearts were darkened.
Although they claimed to be wise, they became fools *and exchanged the glory of the* ***immortal God*** *for images made to look like* ***mortal man*** *and birds and* ***animals*** *and reptiles.*

Secular colleges and universities, almost without exception, teach evolution and are not allowed to teach creation, even as a theory. Why do you think that is?

The Bible clearly states:

Genesis 1:1
In the beginning God created the heavens and the earth.

This statement doesn't try to argue or convince you; it simply states the fact very clearly! "God is the creator of the heavens and earth."

Man, being full of evil, has long wanted to remove God from his life. For if there is no God, there is therefore no judgment and ultimately no accountability. Thus was born "***if it feels good, do it***." If you follow this credo, then good and evil are simply relative. You may decide what is good and what is evil in your own mind. There is no measuring standard. You make it up as you go along through life. Psychobabble, as many call this line of thinking, blames everything evil or wrong on something that affected your life, i.e. where you were raised, how you were raised, who raised you, what your environment was like, etc. But they never seem to come to the realization that the person might be just plain evil.

If you are an intellectual, and do not want to retain God in your thinking, or even worse, think there is no God, the question begs to be asked: "Why are we here, and how did we get here?" As an intellectual, one cannot just let this question go unanswered, for all reasonable people must have some kind of answer for this most important of questions. They reason, and come up with some sort of explanation of how the earth was formed, and how, and why mankind got here.

If you don't believe in God, you might start looking around for an explanation for this age-old question, "Why are we here and Where did we come from?". Some have come up with "scientific" theories, with absolutely no scientific evidence: the big bang, evolution, and natural selection. These so-called "scientific theories" actually are the opposite of all the scientific evidence. You don't have to have a Ph.D. after your name to figure it out; mere common sense can help you to come to the truth.

It is interesting to note that throughout the history of mankind, men from all cultures, civilizations, and peoples believed that they were created and that there was a God or gods of some type

– a higher being. In this day and age, where science and intellectualism reign supreme, the peoples of the earth have come to rely on scientists and intellectuals (who bring us the wonderful products of a scientific age) to be all-knowing, thus having an explanation for everything. They believe that if it can't be proven scientifically, then it's not true or real.

Science Doesn't Know Everything

However, in reality, the scientific community doesn't have a clue about many of the wonders in nature. For example, understanding light and how it works; how birds fly from one continent to another; how fish swim from rivers where they are born out to the oceans and travel thousands of miles and return to the very spot where they were born! This world is full of things science does not understand. Yet most folks look to intellectuals to answer all of the world's problems and questions, even spiritual ones. I heard recently that with one movement of the eyeball your brain makes so many calculations that it would take a Cray super computer 100 years of computing to match what your brain does in seconds.

Evolutionists would have us believe that man evolved from a lower form. We supposedly crawled out of the primordial ooze, walked, and/or flew and eventually evolved into monkeys and then became a human man. It always aggravates me when I am in a museum of science, and the evolution of man is depicted in drawings showing the progression from ape to man and nowhere on the drawing is there a disclaimer: **"there is absolutely no evidence for the idea depicted in this drawing."** They show it as fact! They teach it to our children as fact! So now we have generations of young people who have been misled by these teachers and professors. That's what they believe, because that's what they have been taught.

There are many excellent books and Internet web sites on this subject refuting the evolution myth. A few of the best sites are found on the Internet at: **Understand the Times** http://www.understandthetimes.org, **The Institute for Creation Research** http://www.icr.org,. Many of the men who are the researchers in these organizations are scientists and biologists. Most were, by their own admission, once believers in evolution. But after years of studying the Evolution Model vs. the Creation Model, they have come to the conclusion that the evidence for creation is overwhelming and the theory of evolution won't hold water.

I will not go into this subject in depth here; however, I will cover a few relevant points.

The Myth of Evolution

Let's start by taking a look at transmutation to determine if evolution could really even happen. Let's see if there is any evidence to justify belief in evolution. If any species ever transmuted, one would think there would be evidence in the fossil record.

There is evidence in the fossil record and in nature itself of mutations. Mutation means when a horse changes from a small horse to a larger horse, within the same species. Transmutation is when a cow becomes a horse; it changes species.

We (mankind) have in our possession hundreds of thousands of fossils. The fossil record is very extensive. If evolution is correct and all of the brilliant evolutionary scholars are correct, then it stands to reason that over the millions of years of evolution, and the hundreds of thousands of fossils we have, there would be some fossil, somewhere, just one, that is in the in between stage – transmuting from one species to another. This fossil would show that it is part of one species and part of another; i.e., a reptile that just started to grow wings! In fact, given the huge number of fossils we have, one would think that there would be hundreds, if not thousands, of these in-between examples in the record. Would it surprise you to learn there is **NOT ONE SINGLE** piece of evidence in the entire fossil record that anything ever transmuted? **NOT ONE!** According to the fossil record **NOTHING HAS EVER TRANSMUTED, EVER!** Species simply appear in the fossil record as one species and they remain in that same species. The question begs, just how do all these brilliant scientists come up with the idea we came from lower animals? In all the history of mankind on this earth, until this last century, man believed that a higher being created him. Was that simply superstition, or truth that's merely become very inconvenient to our modern society; a society that craves to fulfill every whim available to them? What makes sense to you?

God Created Everything after its Kind

What does God have to say about species?

Genesis 1:25
And God made the beast of the earth ***after his kind****, and* ***cattle after their kind****, and every thing that creepeth upon the earth* ***after his kind****: and God saw that it was good.*

A horse never mates with a cow, or a cat with a chicken, or a lion with a tiger! Now why is that?

Over and over in Genesis God states that He made everything "***after his kind.***" A horse is never going to become a cow. An ape is never going to become a man.

All the elements have to be present from day one for that entire organism to live or survive. Organs and body parts could not have evolved on their own!

These wise evolutionists would have us believe that things started off in the ooze or slime and over millions of years, through natural selection, things are getting better, improving, evolving.

If evolution was true and we are a result of a cosmic accident and there was no Creator, no God, no judgment, no accountability, then there would be **no real purpose** to life. It really wouldn't matter how you led your life. Think about it.

Follow me on this. There would be no difference between Mother Teresa and Charles Manson. When they died they would simply be "poofed" out of existence, so what would it matter how they lived their lives? One would have lived a selfless life, and the other would have been fully gratified by his wanton lifestyle. One would receive no reward for her sacrifices and the other would receive no punishment for his evil.

If there is no Creator, no one to answer to, you can live your life as you please. If it feels good, do it. Murder, cheat, steal, lie, do good, serve others, live a sacrificial life, lead a good life--it really doesn't matter. Evolution takes away accountability. If people who believe in reincarnation are correct (which they are not), they are admitting that man has a spirit. There would have to be something to return to the next body. If that were true, then who is the force that is redirecting these spirits as they wander around looking for a new body? I've heard it said, "If you won't stand for the truth, you will fall for almost anything." It certainly seems to have proved true.

Second Law of Thermodynamics

Let's take a look at the second law of thermodynamics. This law of science states that **everything** in the known universe is running down, decaying, getting worse. **Not better**.

Evolutionists would have us believe that if we left a pile of bricks in a field, over millions of years and through natural selection these bricks would become a building, or something better; they would evolve.

The second law of thermodynamics states that these bricks left unattended would become dust. Which do you think is more likely—that the bricks will become dust or that they will become a building? Doesn't it make more sense, from what we've all viewed at times in life, that things are running down or decaying? Also, wouldn't it make more sense that you **cannot** have design without a designer!

Take the human body, for example; if nothing else, it is an example of design so far above what intellectual scientists can understand or duplicate. Doctors are known as healers. No doctor ever actually healed anyone, per se. They sew pieces of skin together and God's intricate process heals them. By God's design, our DNA goes to work to replace the cells and repair the damage, and doctors collect the money for it. We never really see the statistics of just how many people, receiving a doctor's care, live and how many die. And you know what? They all die within a few decades, ALL! If you want to look at it that way, doctors (scientists) lose **all** their patients eventually.

Now if the evolutionists were correct, you would expect the world to be evolving into something better. Man himself would be becoming a better creature. Societies would be less corrupt. Civilizations would become more moral. World wide, there would be less crime. World hunger would be on the decline. Wars between nations would be declining. How many of these statements are true in today's world? Can you actually, in your mind's eye, see mankind in the future fulfilling the evolutionist's idea that "everything is getting better, evolving?" This is an idiotic notion at best!

God says in His Word that man was created perfect. He was in a perfect environment; he had everything he would ever need. He also had direct communication with God Himself.

Man sinned against God; he disobeyed Him and became a fallen creature. And he will continue to decline and fall, getting worse until the end of his time on this planet. The Bible makes it clear man is on the way down not on the way up.

Genesis 1:27-30
So God created man in his own image, in the image of God created he him; male and female created he them.

And God blessed them, and God said unto them, be fruitful, and multiply, and replenish the earth, and subdue it: and have dominion over the fish of the sea, and over the fowl of the air, and over every living thing that moveth upon the earth.

And God said, Behold, I have given you every herb bearing seed, which is upon the face of all the earth, and every tree, in the which is the fruit of a tree yielding seed; to you it shall be for meat.

And to every beast of the earth, and to every fowl of the air, and to every thing that creepeth upon the earth, wherein there is life, I have given every green herb for meat: and it was so.

[***Note:*** it's interesting that all things were created for man, not the current politically correct idea that man's purpose is to consider animals much more important than himself.]

Don't you just love the way evolutionists throw around their estimates of time –200 million, 20 billion? They say it like it is true. If you say something authoritatively and as a matter of fact, I guess people are supposed to just believe you. You will hear statements like the dinosaurs lived 70 or 200 million years ago. How are they determining this estimate? There are several ways. One, they date the fossils by the strata where they are found. Of course they date the strata by the fossils that are found in them. What's wrong with this picture? This is circular logic. They have no constant.

How about Carbon 14 Dating?

One of the ways scientists come up with these ridiculous dates is carbon-14 dating. The following is a reprint from the Institute of Creation Research by Dr. John D. Morris:

> *Perhaps no concept in science is as misunderstood as "carbon dating." Almost everyone thinks carbon dating speaks of millions or billions of years. But, carbon dating can't be used to date either rocks or fossils. It is useful only for once-living things that still contain carbon, like flesh or bone or wood. Rocks and fossils, consisting only of inorganic minerals, cannot be dated by this scheme.*

Carbon normally occurs as Carbon-12, but radioactive Carbon-14 may sometimes be formed in the outer atmosphere as Nitrogen-14 undergoes cosmic ray bombardment. The resulting C-14 is unstable and decays back to N-14 with a measured half-life of approximately 5,730 years. Thus the ratio of stable C-12 to unstable C-14, which is known in today's open environment, changes over time in an isolated specimen.

Consider the dating of a piece of wood. As long as the tree lives, it absorbs carbon from the atmosphere in the form of carbon dioxide, both C-12 and C-14. Once the tree dies, it ceases to take in new carbon, and any C-14 present begins to decay. The changing ratio of C-12 to C-14 indicates the length of time since the tree stopped absorbing carbon, i.e., the time of its death.

Obviously, if half the C-14 decays in 5,730 years, and half more decays in another 5,730 years, by ten half-lives (57,300 years) there would be essentially no C-14 left. Thus, no one even considers using carbon dating for dates in this range. In theory, it might be useful to archaeology, but not to geology or paleontology. Furthermore, the assumptions on which it is based and the conditions which must be satisfied are questionable, and in practice, no one trusts it beyond about 3,000 or 4,000 years, and then only if it can be checked by some historical means.

The method assumes, among other things, that the earth's age exceeds the time it would take for C-14 production to be in equilibrium with C-14 decay. Since it would take somewhat less than 50,000 years to reach equilibrium from a world with no C-14 at the start, this always seemed like a good assumption.

That is until careful measurements revealed a significant disequalibrium. The production rate still exceeds decay by 30%. All the present C-14 would accumulate, at present rates of production and build up, in less than 30,000 years! Thus the earth's atmosphere couldn't be any older than this.

Efforts to salvage carbon dating are many and varied, with calibration curves attempting to bring the C-14 "dates" in line with historical dates, but these produce predictably unreliable results.

A "Back to Genesis" way of thinking insists that the Flood of Noah's day would have removed a great deal of the world's carbon from the atmosphere and oceans, particularly as limestone (calcium carbonate) was precipitated. Once the Flood processes ceased, C-14 began a slow build-up to equilibrium with C-12—a build-up not yet complete.

> *Thus carbon dating says nothing at all about millions of years, and often lacks accuracy even with historical specimens, denying as it does the truth of the great Flood. In reality, its measured disequilibrium points to just such a world-altering event, not many years ago.*

As you can see carbon-14 dating is at best unreliable, and at worst just plain wrong.

The Sun and its Mass

Let's consider the sun. It burns off its mass at a measurable rate. One can calculate how long the sun mass would last. Conversely, you can also reverse this formula, and guess what? One hundred million years ago, the sun would occupy the entire solar system! There would be no room for the planets, let alone dinosaurs.

The Grand Canyon

Let's look at the Grand Canyon. The Colorado River runs through the Grand Canyon and it has eroded the ground over the years finally creating the huge canyon. If the river started at the top of the canyon ground, as is believed, the length of time it would take to achieve this would make the earth as we know it today around six thousand years old, not millions of years!

Man's Ancestors according to Science

Let's also look at what else those brilliant scientists have given us.

Again from the Institute of Creation Research and Dr. John D. Morris:

1. *Ramapithecus – a pongid or great ape, not a hominid.*
2. *Piltdown Man – the greatest paleontological hoax.*
3. *Nebraska Man – an extinct pig.*
4. *Cro-Magnon Man – indistinguishable from modern Europeans.*

Homo habilis–- In 1992 Dr. Ian Tattersall stated in 'Evolutionary Anthropology' that: " ... it is increasingly clear that Homo habilis has become a wastebasket taxon, little more than a convenient recipient for a motley assortment of hominid fossils from the latest Pliocene and earliest Pleistocene...."

5. *Neanderthals – Researcher L. A. Yaroch, writing in the 'Yearbook of Physical Anthropolog,', 1996, stated that "the uniqueness of Neanderthals appears to have been exaggerated ..." They were fully human.*
6. *Australopithecus–- In a 1995 biology text published by Prentice Hall, the two authors state: "At the present time, scientists cannot agree on how many species of Australopithecus there were or whether or not they were the ancestors of human beings." Perhaps one reason is that they are so apelike. Upright walking that these creatures may have*

> *engaged in is hardly reason to speculate that they were on the way to becoming human. The living pygmy chimpanzee walks upright. Australopithecus anamensis of Kenya was discovered in August 1995. However, this creature coexisted "4 m.y. ago" with another "early pre-human species" Ardipithecus ramidus, causing "conflicting interpretations" according to 'Worldbook Science Year,' 1997.*

For years the scientific community has tried to feed us its guesses as facts. It always amazed me how they could have a piece of jawbone of one of our "ancestors," and draw a picture of a hairy creature all hunched over dragging its knuckles on the ground. All of that from a piece of jawbone. They must be clairvoyant!

So in conclusion, if we did not crawl out of the ooze and we were created, and there is a God, why should we believe the Bible is the blueprint, telling us how we should live and what happens to us when we die? Is there a heaven and how do we get there? Is there a hell, and if so, how do we stay out of it?

As we continue, we will cover each and every one of these topics.

Chapter 2

Is the Bible the Word of God?

Why is the Bible the Real Authority?

There are probably hundreds, possibly thousands of different religions on the earth. What makes the Bible the real authority?

Let's start by examining this book and how it came to be. Some forty different authors wrote these sixty-six books over a 1500 to 2000 year period. Now let's look at these forty authors. Some were prophets, some were kings and leaders, some were free men, and some were enslaved in captivity. Many of them were educated. Some were not. Yet there is one theme running through the entire Bible. How is that possible?

How many Bibles are in print? More Bibles have been printed than any other book in history. It may be that more Bibles have been printed than all other books combined. For thousands of years mankind has turned to the Bible (the Word of God) for answers to life's questions. They've turned to this book for inspiration, in time of need, or when facing death. People from all walks of life have sought this book: rich men, poor men, kings, peasants, educated and uneducated men and women alike. If there was nothing to this book, if it is just a book of fables, it's certainly quite interesting that so many millions, possibly billions, of people over the centuries have turned to it, relied on it, and believed it, many even went to their deaths because of it. Were these millions of people just stupid, or uninformed, or did they possibly find the truth in this book?

The Bible is the most reliable book ever written. There are more copies that are close to the originals than any other book. This book is more accurate than any other book.

The Dead Sea Scrolls

When the Dead Sea Scrolls were discovered in 1947. Among the artifacts was the complete Book of Isaiah. It was a thousand years older than the oldest copy previously known. In comparing the two, they were virtually identical. Have you ever tried to pass a story or joke around a circle of friends, perhaps ten people? By the time it gets around the circle, it's a different story altogether!

The technique used by the scribes to copy the Word of God is very interesting. Each Hebrew or Greek letter has a numerical equivalent. A=1, B=2, etc. When a scribe copied a page, he would count up the total of the numerical value of the letters in the original text and then count up the total on his newly copied page. If the totals did not equal, he would throw away his copied page and start over again. The emphasis on accuracy was everything. If it was not a perfect copy, it was worthless. Also, these men did not read a sentence and then write it from memory. They looked at one letter at a time, copied it, and repeated that step. This method was very accurate and few mistakes were made. If the king entered the room when a scribe was working on the Scriptures, he did not have to look up or bow to pay homage to the king. That was the only time anyone could ignore the king and live. Thus, this insured accuracy as well. We all know what interruptions do to our focus and accuracy. They knew that their work was so very important, copying God's Word, that strict rules were followed at all times.

All of the foregoing facts are interesting; however, they are not the main proof of the authenticity of the Bible.

God Exists outside of the Time Domain

God has a unique quality. He exists outside of time. He lives in eternity. Though we don't really understand this concept, God tells us that He sees all of time, the beginning to the end. So God can speak of the future as though it has already happened. This is called prophecy in the Bible. Only God has the ability to speak of the future before it happens. This is what really distinguishes the Bible over all other religious books and writings of so-called prophets. We will cover this in detail in chapter 4.

I'm sure we've all tried to contemplate eternity. I believe we do not have the capacity to understand the concept. However, it's interesting to consider concepts like eternity from time to time.

In thinking about eternity, let us consider the following: if one were in eternity, there would be no past. You would never think about yesterday. There is no future. You would never plan for anything, look forward to anything. You are living in the continuing NOW only. It's a hard concept to contemplate, mind-boggling really. Some day when we get there we will have the capacity to understand. That is reassuring.

There are many scholarly works that delve deep into the subject of the reliability of the Bible. I would encourage everyone to spend as much time as it takes to be well-versed in this most important subject. Again, what amount of time and effort should a person invest in his or her own everlasting eternity?

Chapter 3

God's Plan for Man

The Love Story

The Bible is a love story. It's a story about God who created a world and all things surrounding it. He created man (in His own image and likeness) for the **purpose of fellowship**. He gave man everything he needed for his well-being. Man was given dominion over all the earth, including all the creatures on the earth. He was given the "Title Deed to the Earth" so to speak. This was his place, his domain.

God Himself actually fellowshipped with man face-to-face in the environment He had created. Man was created **body**, **soul** and **spirit**. Man's spirit is what enables him to communicate with God. The Bible says God is Spirit. In order for man to demonstrate his love for God, man was given a free will, that if he chose to, man could make a choice not to love or obey God. God would honor man's decision according to his free will. This would ultimately cost God and mankind a very high price.

Why would God give man free will? I believe free will was given to show **man** whether or not he really loved God. (God is all-knowing; you can't show God anything.) The only way to do that was to give man an opportunity to rebel and disobey, thus showing that man did not love or trust God.

God created man for fellowship, to love man and have man love Him. There can be no real love, unless the object of love has the ability to not love in return, thus free will. In order for man to love God, he had to have the right to not love God

Man's Demonstration of his Love toward God

How would man initially demonstrate his love for God? He would obey God, thus showing that he loved and trusted God. God had his best interest at heart.

When Adam lived in the Garden of Eden, he was told that he could freely partake of any of the trees in the garden for his food. There was only one exception, one law, so to speak. He was not to eat from the tree that was in the center of the garden – the Tree of the Knowledge of Good and Evil. Can you imagine a world with only ONE LAW? By keeping this one law or commandment, Adam could express his love and trust for God.

As with all laws from God, this one was given for man's benefit. Man in this original state knew nothing about the difference between good and evil. It was not in his vocabulary or understanding. God knew that Adam did not need to know about evil to live a full and happy life. Think of what kind of world would come from only good. Some would say that would be called Paradise.

Bad News for Mankind

There was another creature in the Garden. His original name was Lucifer, son of the morning. He was a created being, the most perfect and beautiful creature God had ever created. So this was part of God's creation prior to man. There are some that think that before man's creation the earth was somehow under the dominion of Lucifer. Lucifer was not just another angelic being. He was *numero uno*, number one. He was the highest ranking cherub, probably first in command of all created beings, second only to God Himself.

Lucifer did not want to be under anyone or to be accountable to anyone. He wanted to "do his own thing." He wanted to answer to no one but himself. He wanted to be the supreme ruler. Does that attitude sound familiar?

There is more going on here, in the garden, than you might pick up on at first glance. When Satan (formerly Lucifer – his pre-fall name) tempted Eve and she ate of the Tree of the Knowledge of Good and Evil, Adam ate with her. They both disobeyed God and broke the one law, the only commandment God had given them.

The Title Deed Passes from Man to Satan

As a result of this transgression, God drove Adam and Eve from the Garden of Eden, and they had to fend for themselves. The actual **Title Deed** of the earth was taken from them and given to

Satan. Because of their actions Satan became the ruler of this world, the god of this world, so to speak. How do we know this? When Jesus was tempted by Satan in the Judean desert, one of the temptations was that he (Satan) would give Jesus "all the kingdoms of this world, if He would just bow down and worship him."

Luke 4:5-8
Then the devil, taking Him up on a high mountain, showed Him all the kingdoms of the world in a moment of time. And the devil said to Him, "All this authority I will give You, and their glory; ***for this has been delivered to me, and I give it to whomever I wish.***
Therefore, if You will worship before me, all will be Yours."

Jesus did not dispute the fact that all these kingdoms belong to Satan to give to whomever he willed.

[***Note:*** I believe many people over the centuries have said YES to this same temptation and been given their own kingdom of this world! Jesus answering Satan's temptation by declaring He would worship God only. It's definitely not healthy to worship Satan.]

Mark 8:36
For what shall it profit a man, if he shall gain the whole world, and lose his own soul?

All the kingdoms of this world do not give one access to heaven and the kingdom of God.

Jesus on another occasion said:

Matthew 19:24
And again I say unto you, It is easier for a camel to go through the eye of a needle, than for ***a rich man to enter into the kingdom of God****.*

Why do you think God would say this? Is He down on rich folks? Hardly, the Bible says that God is not a respecter of persons. He loves all people the same. Why is it then that He would make such a statement?

Matthew 6:19-21
Do not lay up for yourselves treasures on earth, where moth and rust destroy and where thieves break in and steal; but lay up for yourselves ***treasures in heaven****, where neither moth nor rust destroys and where thieves do not break in and steal.*
For where your treasure is, there your heart will be also .

Wherever you invest your time, money, and your love, that's where your heart is! Generally speaking a rich man's time, thoughts, energy and, yes, worship are focused on his wealth, so that's where his heart is. However, it is possible to be rich and also be one of God's children. It just isn't easy to achieve.

Jesus is the Second Adam (a Kinsman Redeemer)

Jesus is often referred to as "the second Adam." What Adam could not accomplish as the "first Adam," Jesus did accomplish as the "second Adam." Sin came to all mankind because of what Adam did (the first Adam), likewise salvation can come to all men because of what Jesus (the second Adam) did.

When all this happened back in the Garden of Eden, God made a promise.

Genesis 3:14-15

And the LORD God said unto the serpent, Because thou hast done this, thou art cursed above all cattle, and above every beast of the field; upon thy belly shalt thou go, and dust shalt thou eat all the days of thy life:

And I will ***put enmity between thee and the woman, and*** ***between thy seed*** *and* ***her seed****; it shall bruise thy head, and thou shalt bruise his heel.*

This is the first promise of a savior. The seed of the woman and the seed of the serpent (Satan) are contrasted in Genesis. It's interesting to note that Satan has seed (offspring)! That's a scary thought, isn't it?

I'm sure God would just like to excuse man for his transgression, just like we would excuse one of our children. However, God is not a fallen being and His character is not like men in this respect. God is holy and perfectly righteous. This is a concept that man, in his fallen state has trouble grasping.

Was there any way to save mankind? God's righteous character demanded that the transgression would have to be made right. Someone would have to pay for all the sin and wrongdoing of mankind. Who could possibly qualify to do this? It would have to be someone that was totally sinless just as Adam was before the Fall.

This was a project that only God Himself could accomplish. God in His own wisdom, because he loved man so deeply and dearly, decided only He, God, could redeem the world. This is the ultimate gift to man, demonstrating just how much God loves man.

This reminds me of a story I heard once. There was a man who had a son he loved dearly. It was a gift-giving time, like Christmas, and he purchased a wonderful gift for his grown son. This gift cost him everything he had. When he offered his son the gift, the son would not accept it and just set it aside. For years and years the gift just sat there, unopened. How do you think this would make the father feel?

God has given us the gift of eternal life. What are you doing with it? Have you just set it aside?

The Bible states that there is only one God. However, God manifests Himself in three different personalities. The Father, Son and the Holy Spirit. The Son would become the second Adam, so to speak, and bear the sins of all mankind and become the savior of man.

However, there was one more qualification for a redeemer of mankind, the redeemer had to be a human being, a man, an ancestor of Adam. Only a **kinsman redeemer** of Adam's race, as the Bible puts it, could qualify. This is what the Book of Ruth is all about. It is the picture of a kinsman redeemer.

So God Himself, in the person of the Son, would have to give up His throne and glory and become a man. How could the God of the universe leave all that glory and power and pay the price of man's sin? Can you see the depth of God's love for man? This would make man "right" with God again, as in the beginning. God the Father would choose the proper time in man's history to bring His Son the Redeemer into this world.

Jesus is the Living Word of God

John 1:1-5
In the beginning was the Word, (Jesus, the God the Son) and the Word was with God, and the ***Word was God****. He was in the beginning with God. All things were made through Him, and without Him nothing was made that was made. In Him was life, and the life was the light of men. And the light shines in the darkness, and the darkness did not comprehend it.*

John 1:14-15
And the Word became flesh and dwelt among us*, and we beheld His glory, the glory as of the only begotten of the Father,* ***full of grace and truth****.*

Have you ever had a child who was sick and hurting? You would gladly take the illness on yourself rather than see your child suffer. How could God let His children, created in His likeness, suffer in sin, being separated from God forever? God in His love for mankind had to fix this situation, had to redeem His children and His entire creation. He had to take the sin and disobedience of mankind upon Himself just like we would for our child, if we were able to do so.

This is what the entire Bible is about, the fall of man, and redemption of mankind by God. It is a love story. God so loved man that He became a man Himself, because only God Himself could make this transgression right

John 10:27-31
My sheep hear My voice, and I know them, and they follow Me.
And I give them eternal life, and they shall never perish; neither shall anyone snatch them out of My hand.
My Father, who has given them to Me, is greater than all; and no one is able to snatch them out of My Father's hand.
I and My Father are one.
Then the Jews took up stones again to stone Him .

The religious Jews knew what Jesus was claiming, ***"I and My Father are one."*** He was definitely God, and they wanted to stone Him, as it was a capital offense to claim to be God or equal with God.

As we start reading the Bible, we soon see that after his fall in the garden, man became more and more corrupt and evil. Of course, he had a little help from the ruler of darkness, the ruler of this world – Satan.

God Communicates His Word to Future Generations

There was a dilemma however; how would subsequent generations of mankind know God's character, His love for man? He would have to reveal Himself to man. How?
A holy God cannot communicate directly with sinful man. God's plan was to choose a man (Abraham). This man's ancestors would become a nation (Israel). He would reveal Himself to these people and they in turn would reveal God to all of mankind.

The entire Bible is about God moving through human beings to save mankind.

On the other hand, God's adversary, Satan only has one goal, to stop God's plan for the redemption of mankind. He will do anything to take all of mankind where he is going to end up, and it's not a good place, to say the least.

You know it has always bothered me, ever since I became a Christian, how Satan, a created being, could possibly think that he could win in a battle with the God who created him and everything else in the universe. I think God has given me some insight into this question. We know from the Scripture, Satan is a very vain and intelligent creature. I've always wondered, What is he (Satan) thinking? Or what is his plan to think he can win against God? What is the one thing that could limit an all-powerful God? His Word! I believe Satan thinks he is going to out-smart God, based on the promises of His written Word. I personally think this is ludicrous and idiotic on Satan's part. However, look at how intellectuals tend to look at things; Satan is the ultimate intellectual.

Man was so corrupt at one point that God considered wiping out the entire human race. He decided to save eight souls only, a man named Noah and his family. They were the survivors of the Flood. So when someone asks you, "Where are you from?" we can all say, "Originally from Turkey" - that's where the ark landed.

When man was in the Garden of Eden, it appears that he communicated with God on a spiritual level. Man's spirit communed with God's Spirit. Man lost that part of himself, his spirit, in the Fall. Thus the Bible speaks of man being spiritually dead after the Fall. Man could not commune with God any longer face-to-face on a one-to-one level. God would rarely communicate with man face-to-face. On the rare occasions that He did, He assumed the form of a man. So as the generations of man continued, how would they know of God's plan for man's redemption?

God needed a conduit through which He could reveal His plan. God started revealing His answer to man's sin. His redeemer, the savior of mankind would come at the proper time. This is what the Bible is all about. Jesus the Son of God speaking:

Jesus Said of the Scriptures

John 5:39-40
You search the Scriptures, for in them you think you have eternal life; and ***these are they which testify of Me***.

Hebrews 10:7
Then I said, 'Behold, I have come--
In the volume of the book it is written of Me–
To do Your will, O God.'

Abram, God's Man of the Hour

God chose a man, Abram. Abram was a sinner and idol worshipper, but ***he believed God*** and it was ***accounted unto him for righteousness.***
Remember this **"Belief or Faith = Righteousness".**

God told Abram to separate himself from his people, and thus God started working with a single man, who later became a people, and even later became a nation. He revealed His redemption plan to them to carry to all of mankind. God through the dealings with this man and later his descendants would give example after example of His character, His Love and His plan for mankind. He gave this group of people, later to be called the nation of Israel and later the Jews, His law. Now the law was given to man for man's benefit. If he would keep God's law, he would have good success, and prosper, and all would go well for man. Jesus said that the whole law could be summarized in just two statements:

Matthew 22:37-40

`Love the Lord your God with all your heart and with all your soul and with all your mind.' This is the first and greatest commandment. And the second is like it: `Love your neighbor as yourself.' All the Law and the Prophets hang on these two commandments.

He said, "In these two commandments are a summation of all of the Law." If you keep these commandments, you will prosper and have good success and please God.

Through the prophets of Israel, God began to reveal Himself, His character and His plan for the redemption of mankind.

If you were God, just how could you authenticate this message? You could not have direct contact with man any longer because of your holiness, purity and righteousness and the fact man was dead spiritually.

God who lives in eternity, outside of the time domain, can authenticate His message in a way no one else can. Since God can see from the beginning to the end, all events in time at one glance, He has a foolproof way of doing this. He can write down future events in advance, in a book. It is estimated that more than 25% of the Bible is prophecy. Now at this point in time, much of this prophecy has been fulfilled. So we can look at the fulfilled prophecies and know for sure that this book was inspired from outside the time domain. We can look at future prophecies and know for sure they will come to pass exactly as they are written.

God is Outside of Time

I'll give an illustration I heard recently. Let's look at a road as though it were all of time for the purpose of this illustration.

If you were sitting on Main Street (which we will call a certain point in time), the street represents all of time, and you are watching a series of old cars go by. A bystander comes up to you and asks if the '49 Ford had come by yet. You say, "Yes it did – about five minutes ago." He says, "Darn, I wanted to see that car." You could tell him, "If you hurry, you can proceed to the next intersection and see the '49 Ford." He would be going into the **future** to see the **past**. Suppose he asks, "Has the '38 Buick come by yet?" You could tell him, "No, it's about five minutes away from here." He could go back down the block to see this car. He would be going into the **past** to see the **future**.

Now let's say God is in a blimp overhead and can see the entire road or all of time. In His point of view, he can see the '38 Buick approaching a given point in time and He can see the '49 Ford that has already passed that point in time, so He could write about the future events as though they had already happened. Prophecy!

What Separates Jesus from All Others

Prophecy and the Resurrection of Jesus Christ are what separate the God of the Bible and Judeo/Christianity from all other forms of religion. All the others have good teachings, great sayings; however, only God can speak of the future in advance. All the other prophets or "holy men" are in their graves. Only one, Jesus the Son of God, has conquered death; His tomb is empty.

Mohammed died of illness. Islam is based on Mohammed's teachings. Buddha died of natural causes. Buddhism is based on Buddha's teachings. Jesus was crucified for our sin and was resurrected from the dead. Christianity is based on what a man actually did. See the difference?

Much of the Bible is painting a picture of God, His personality, His character, His nature. We, as human beings, descendants of Adam, can actually know the character of God. We can trust God. If God says something, we can believe it.

Titus 1:1-3
..., which God, who does not lie, promised before the beginning of time, and at his appointed season he brought his word to light through the preaching entrusted to me by the command of God our Savior,

You have to know someone before you can believe anything he says.

Knowing is Believing

A pastor friend put it this way: Suppose someone approached you on the street, pointed at the building in front of you and said to you, "I am going to give you this building." You would think, "Yeah, right!" You would have a very difficult time believing this man–wouldn't you agree?

Then as time passed you found out a little more about this man. You found out he actually owns this building. Now you think, perhaps he is going to give me this building. It is a little easier to believe. It is now coming into the realm of possibility.

Then you discover a little more about this man. He owns the entire block of buildings. Wow, now it becomes even more probable he might really give you this building. Then you find out he owns the entire town, every building in it. Now it is very possible you might be the new owner of this building. You're excited. Then comes more information; you find out he owns the whole world. Now you become convinced he will give you this building.

Can you see the progression? The more you know about this man, the easier it is to believe what he has promised.

This is the formula God has used in the Bible. Before you can believe Him, you have to know who He is and know His character. The more you know, the easier it is to believe.

It's sad that so many people say they don't believe what God has said in His Word. In reality, they don't know the first thing about God or His ways. They are like the person on the street and the man has just promised to give him the building. Since they don't know the man, they don't believe he will do it. Now suppose the only condition to receive the building is that you believe he will do it. If you never investigate the man and find out about him, you will probably never receive the building, because it will be impossible for you to believe.

God in His love for mankind laid out a road map of laws. He did not give them to him to torture man, or deprive him of the good things of this life. He gave them to man to make man's stay on this planet more enjoyable. If you keep these laws, they will help you. They will be good for you.

Father Knows Best

A father always knows what's best for his children. Suppose your small child wanted to play with a large kitchen knife, because to her it looked shiny and pretty, and she thinks it would be a desirable thing to play with. She would say, "Daddy, I want to play with the large shiny knife!" You would immediately say, "NO!" She of course would say, "Why"? You would say, "Because I said so!" Now if she loves and trusts you completely, knowing that you only have her best interest at heart, she would say, "Okay, Dad." If she says, "I want to play with the shiny knife anyway," you would immediately understand she doesn't know or realize you have her best interest at heart. She does not have faith in you. You would be disappointed with her, and would probably be a little sad she doesn't have more trust in you concerning her welfare.

How does man respond? Instead of trusting God and keeping His laws, he goes his own direction. He does not keep the laws of God and he pays the price. He plays with the sharp knife and suffers the consequences.

If you want to know what that price is, look around you. Take a look at the world. That's the price man is paying everyday!

Man, in his rebellion against God and His laws, has pretty much messed up this planet. We love to blame God for everything. When some disaster strikes, we say it was an "Act of God," laying the blame squarely on God. In reality, it is the consequences of man's rebellion. We would be more correct to declare this to be the result of a rebellious act of man, not God.

You cannot believe what God has to say unless you first learn who God is, and what is His character.

God is Love

What is the character of God? The Bible says God is love.

I John 4:7-8
*Dear friends, let us love one another, for love comes from God. Everyone who loves has been born of God and knows God. Whoever does not love does not know God, because **God is love**.*

I John 4:16

And so we know and rely on the love God has for us. God is love. Whoever lives in love lives in God, and God in him.

God's motives toward man are good; they are thoughts of love, from a loving God.

But ultimately God will respect our free will. If we are determined to exercise our free will to sin and go our own way, the path to destruction and the one that leads to hell, God will respect our free will decision.

God Gives Lesson after Lesson to Man

For thousands of years, God, through His people Israel (and later through the Christians) has given lesson after lesson, metaphors and examples of how we should live and relate to God and to each other. He inspired man to write them in a book, so future generations could also know these lessons. God would reveal these truths to one group of people in history who would eventually reveal them to all generations. The proof of authenticity that the Bible is a true representation of God speaking to man is Bible prophecy, the future written in advance. God and God alone knows the future before it happens.

2 Peter 1:21

for prophecy never came by the will of man, but holy men of God spoke as they were moved by the Holy Spirit.

The Bible was not written by man's intelligence, but by men of God, as the Holy Spirit of God inspired them. Every word, every letter, every space is the inerrant word of God.

How Big is Your God?

Let's look at this with just plain common sense. Say there is a God, the God of the Bible. He is all-powerful, all-knowing. He made the world and the heavens and everything that is in them! If this God is all-powerful and almighty, and He wanted to reveal Himself to man whom He had created, don't you think He would be powerful enough to do just that? If God wanted to reveal Himself, do you really think little puny man could stop Him? I personally don't think so. However, there is one who wants to sow seeds of doubt, or confusion, thereby causing disbelief. He is the enemy of God and of mankind alike.

I'm sure Adam passed his knowledge of man and the history of mankind down to his children verbally. In time, God gave Moses His Ten Commandments; it was also given to Moses to write the history of the descendants of Adam and Abraham and the Law of God. This was faithfully passed from generation to generation. Along the way God raised up prophets, men of God, to write down instructions, warnings and prophecies of God's plan for the redemption of mankind.

God says throughout the Old Testament that He would send a deliverer, a Messiah. There are some 300 prophecies of the coming Messiah. There is a prophecy in Daniel 9 predicting the very day the Messiah would come. We will go into that prophecy in detail in a subsequent chapter.

The ultimate goal of God is to bring man back to where he started, into close fellowship with Himself. This is a process that only God can accomplish. Man in all his efforts, all his good religious works, cannot accomplish this. The redemption of man is the work of God alone.

Ephesians 2:7-10
For by grace you have been ***saved through faith****, and that not of yourselves; it is the gift of God****, not of works****, lest anyone should boast. For we are His workmanship, created in Christ Jesus for good works, which God prepared beforehand that we should walk in them.*

Chapter 4.

The Proof of the Bible (Prophecy)

Prophecy

As we have mentioned in the foregoing chapters, the ultimate proof of the authenticity of the Bible is prophecy. This is the facet of Christianity that sets itself apart from all other religions.

It is estimated that the Bible is actually close to 25% prophecy. Many of the prophecies of the Bible have already come to pass, thereby authenticating the Bible itself. However, there are hundreds of prophecies that have not yet taken place, which gives those who have studied and learned of these a chance to see them fulfilled in the future. There are, of course, numerous subtle prophecies. We will be looking at a few of the major ones.

The Coming Messiah

It is estimated that there are 300 direct prophecies in the Old Testament of the first coming of the Messiah, Jesus. The mathematical odds of one man being born and fulfilling just 20 of these prophecies is a number with 57 zeros after it. In other words, mathematically impossible! Yet Jesus fulfilled them all. Wouldn't you consider this a major point of proof that He is who He claimed to be?

As we mentioned before, from the very beginning God promised a deliverer, a man who would redeem the human race. A Messiah!

However, as we look at the pictures that the Old Testament prophecies paint of the Messiah, we see that He is to play two entirely different roles. One picture is as the Suffering Messiah who comes to earth as a man who would pay the price for man's sin in His own body. The other is of a man who would come as the King of Kings, a warrior-king, and He would defeat Israel's enemies and set up God's Kingdom on earth. The reason the majority of the Jewish people living in Israel at the time of Jesus missed the Messiah was that they were disregarding the prophecies of the suffering Messiah in favor of the king Messiah. They so wanted the Messiah to throw off the bondage of Rome and to free the Israelite people that they flat overlooked the Scriptures that He had to come first to pay the price for our sins as part of the redemption scenario.

Chief among these prophecies is Isaiah 53, the first coming of the Messiah from the Old Testament.

Isaiah 53

Who has believed our report? And to whom has the arm of the LORD been revealed?

For He shall grow up before Him as a tender plant, and as a root out of dry ground. He has no form or comeliness; and when we see Him, there is no beauty that we should desire Him.

He is despised and rejected by men, a Man of sorrows and acquainted with grief. And we hid, as it were, our faces from Him; he was despised, and we did not esteem Him.
Surely ***He has borne our griefs and carried our sorrows****; yet we esteemed Him stricken, smitten by God, and afflicted.*
But He was wounded for our transgressions, he was bruised for our iniquities*; the chastisement for our peace was upon Him, and by His stripes we are healed.*
All we like sheep have gone astray; we have turned, every one, to his own way; and ***the LORD has laid on Him the iniquity of us all.***
*He was oppressed and He was afflicted, yet He opened not His mouth****; he was led as a lamb to the slaughter****, and as a sheep before its shearers is silent, so He opened not His mouth.*
He was taken from prison and from judgment, and who will declare His generation? For He was cut off from the land of the living; ***for the transgressions of My people He was stricken.***
And they made His grave with the wicked-- but with the rich at His death, because He ***had done no violence, nor was any deceit in His mouth****.*
Yet it pleased the LORD to bruise Him; he has put Him to grief. When You make His soul ***an offering for sin****, he shall see His seed, He shall prolong His days, and the pleasure of the LORD shall prosper in His hand.*
He shall see the labor of His soul, and be satisfied. ***By His knowledge My righteous Servant shall justify many, for He shall bear their iniquities****.*
Therefore I will divide Him a portion with the great, and He shall divide the spoil with the strong, because ***He poured out His soul unto death****, and He was numbered with the*

transgressors, and ***He bore the sin of many, and made intercession for the transgressors***.

The Second Coming of the Messiah

The following is the prophecy of the second coming of the Messiah from the New Testament.

Revelations 19:11-16
Now I saw heaven opened, and behold, a white horse. And He who sat on him was called Faithful and True, and in righteousness He judges and makes war.
His eyes were like a flame of fire, and on His head were many crowns. He had a name written that no one knew except Himself.
He was clothed with a robe dipped in blood (of his enemies*), and His name is called The Word of God* ***[Jesus from John 1:1].***
And the armies in heaven, clothed in fine linen, white and clean, followed Him on white horses.
Now out of His mouth goes a sharp sword [the Word of God], *that with it He should strike the nations. And He Himself* ***will rule them with a rod of iron****. He Himself treads the winepress of* ***the fierceness and wrath of Almighty God.***
*And He has on His robe and on His thigh a name written****: KING OF KINGS AND LORD OF LORDS.***

The Day of His Coming Foretold

Probably the most significant prophecy in the Bible about the Messiah is the prediction of the very day that He would enter into the city of Jerusalem and proclaim Himself as King!

This prophecy can be found in Daniel 9:24. It relates to an earlier incident in Leviticus 25:3 when God told His people that they were to work the land for six years, and the seventh year they should not work the land as it was a Sabbath year. They were required to let the land rest.

Leviticus 25: 3-4
Six years you shall sow your field, and six years you shall prune your vineyard, and gather its fruit; but in the ***seventh year there shall be a Sabbath*** *of solemn rest for the land, a Sabbath to the LORD.*

However, the people of Israel did not obey God (does this sound familiar?); they did not keep the Sabbath year for 490 years.

God said, "You owe Me seventy years of Sabbaths." This is why the children of Israel were taken into captivity by King Nebuchadnezzar to fulfill and pay back these seventy years of Sabbaths. This all happened during the life of the prophet Daniel.

One day Daniel was praying and seeking God.

Daniel 9:20-23
Now while I was speaking, praying, and confessing my sin and the sin of my people Israel, and presenting my supplication before the LORD my God for the holy mountain of my God, yes, while I was speaking in prayer, the man Gabriel, whom I had seen in the vision at the beginning, being caused to fly swiftly, reached me about the time of the evening offering. And he informed me, and talked with me, and said, ***"O Daniel, I have now come forth to give you skill to understand. At the beginning of your supplications the command went out, and I have come to tell you, for you are greatly beloved; therefore consider the matter, and <u>understand the vision</u>:"***

Let's take a look at Daniel 9:24. This is what the angel Gabriel said to Daniel:

Daniel 9:24-10:1
Seventy weeks are determined
For your people and for your holy city,
To finish the transgression,
To make an end of sins,
To make reconciliation for iniquity,
To bring in everlasting righteousness,
To seal up vision and prophecy,
And to anoint the Most Holy.

Know therefore and understand,
That from the going forth of the command
To restore and build Jerusalem
Until Messiah the Prince,

There shall be seven weeks and sixty-two weeks;
The street shall be built again, and the wall,
Even in troublesome times.

And after the sixty-two weeks
Messiah shall be cut off, but not for Himself;
And the people of the Prince who is to come
Shall destroy the city and the sanctuary.
The end of it shall be with a flood,
And till the end of the war desolations are determined.
Then he shall confirm a covenant with many for one week;
But in the middle of the week
He shall bring an end to sacrifice and offering.
And on the wing of abominations shall be one who makes desolate,
Even until the consummation, which is determined,
Is poured out on the desolate.

The Seventieth Week of Daniel

When these seventy weeks were complete, this would usher in the kingdom of God. These seventy weeks are actually seventy weeks of years and would accomplish seven things.

1. *To finish the transgression,* **(the 490 years of not keeping the Sabbath)**
2. *To make an end of sins,* **(to bring an end of sin on the earth, i.e. Adam's transgression)**

3. *To make reconciliation for iniquity,* **(Christ paid the price for our sins)**
4. *To bring in everlasting righteousness,* **(to bring the world into conformity with God's Kingdom)**
5. *To seal up vision*
6. *And prophecy,* **(to fulfill all the prophecies of the Bible)**
7. *And to anoint the Most Holy.* **(to crown Jesus as King or as some think to anoint the Holy Place)**

These seven things would bring an end to this world as we know it. Let's look further.

Daniel 9:25
Know therefore and understand,
That from the going forth of the command
To restore and build Jerusalem
Until Messiah the Prince,
There shall be seven weeks and sixty-two weeks;

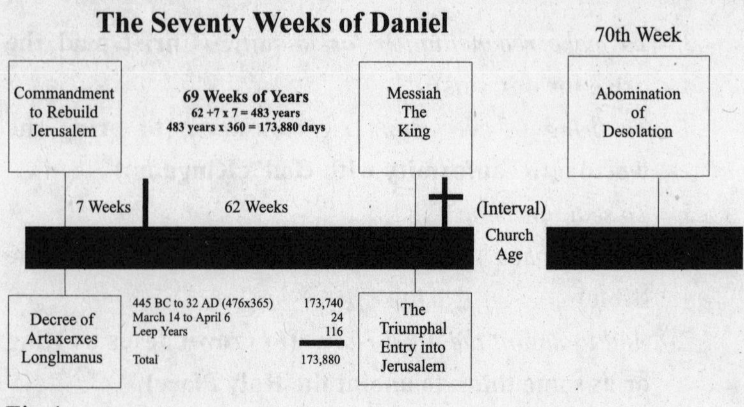

Fig 1

The street shall be built again, and the wall,
Even in troublesome times.

The idiom of "week" of years was common in Israel in those days.

From secular history we know the commandment to restore and rebuild Jerusalem was given by King Artaxerxes Longimanus on March 14, 445 B.C. This is the starting point; the Bible says from that day forward we count 173,880 days and the Messiah would present Himself to Jerusalem.

If you follow carefully the life of Jesus, you will see that on numerous occasions they tried to worship Him and make Him king. He continually told them, "No, don't do that. My time is not yet." Until one day He specifically sets up a scenario. He tells two disciples to go and a get a young donkey (unbroken). He tells them that if the owner asks why they want it to tell him,

“The Master has need of it.” He sits on this unbroken donkey (a miracle) and starts to ride on the road from Bethany to Jerusalem, fulfilling
Zechariah 9:9.

Zechariah 9:9
Behold, your King is coming to you;
He is just and having ***salvation****,*
Lowly and riding on a donkey,
A colt, the foal of a donkey.

The people were lining up on both sides of the road singing a psalm. It was Psalm 118. It was understood by the Jews in general, and especially by the Jewish leadership, that this psalm was to be sung only when the true Messiah presented Himself to the people! That’s why the Jewish leaders came to Jesus and demanded that He get the crowd to stop proclaiming Him as the awaited Jewish Messiah.

Luke 19:37-40
Then, as He was now drawing near the descent of the Mount of Olives, the whole multitude of the disciples began to rejoice and praise God with a loud voice for all the mighty works they had seen, saying:

"Blessed is the King who comes in the name of the LORD!"
Peace in heaven and glory in the highest!

And some of the Pharisees called to Him from the crowd, "Teacher, rebuke Your disciples." But He answered and said to

them, "I tell you that if these should keep silent, the stones would immediately cry out."

The Day Jesus Enters Jerusalem as King!

This was April 6, A.D. 32 -- 173,880 days since King Artaxerxes Longimanus gave the commandment to restore and rebuild Jerusalem--the very day predicted centuries before by the prophet Daniel to be the day the Jewish Messiah would present Himself as King.

As the illustration (Figure 1) shows, this paid back sixty-nine weeks of years that Israel owed to God. However, it still left one week of years, or seven years, owed to God by the Jews.

Daniel 9:26-10:1
And after the sixty-two weeks
Messiah shall be cut off, but not for Himself;
And the people of the prince who is to come
Shall destroy the city and the sanctuary.
The end of it shall be with a flood,
And till the end of the war desolations are determined.

Verse 26 states that the Messiah will be "cut off" (killed). "And the people of the Prince (Antichrist, or false messiah) who is to come shall destroy the city and the sanctuary and the end shall be with a flood" (dispersion). Which is exactly what happened in A.D. 70. The Jewish people lost their homeland and were scattered around the world. It would be 2000 years until they would return to their land, Israel.

Now this leaves the seven years left to accomplish the seven items we discussed.

1. *To finish the transgression,*
2. *To make an end of sins,*
3. *To make reconciliation for iniquity,*
4. *To bring in everlasting righteousness,*
5. *To seal up vision*
6. *and prophecy,*
7. *And to anoint the Most Holy.*

As of this writing, these things have not yet been accomplished. We still have sin and iniquity and it is obvious that "everlasting righteousness" has not yet arrived.

There is this matter of the seven years still owed to God by the Jewish people. You will notice in the illustration, a gap after the Crucifixion of Jesus Christ. God has put aside the Jewish people and has given the Gentiles a chance to evangelize the world. However, God is not yet done with the Jews. At some point in the future, God is going to remove His church from the earth as written in 1 Thessalonians 4:16 and 1 Corinthians 15:50. This is commonly referred to as the "Rapture" (from the Latin Vulgate) of the church.

The Rapture of the Church

1 Thessalonians 4:16-17

For the Lord Himself will descend from heaven with a shout, with the voice of an archangel, and with the trumpet of God. And the dead in Christ will rise first. Then we who are alive and remain shall **be caught up together with them in the clouds** *to meet the Lord in the air. And thus we shall always be with the Lord.*

1 Corinthians 15:50-54

Now this I say, brethren, that flesh and blood cannot inherit the kingdom of God; nor does corruption inherit incorruption. Behold, I tell you a mystery: We shall not all sleep,(die) but we shall all be changed-- in a moment, in the twinkling of an eye, at the last trumpet. For the trumpet will sound, and the dead will be raised incorruptible, and we shall be changed. For this corruptible must put on incorruption, and this mortal must put on immortality. So when this corruptible has put on incorruption, and this mortal has put on immortality, then shall be brought to pass the saying that is written: "Death is swallowed up in victory."

Then he shall confirm a covenant with many for one week **[seven years];**
But in the middle of the week **[three and a half years]**
He shall bring an end to sacrifice and offering.
And on the wing of abominations shall be one who makes desolate,
Even until the consummation, which is determined,
Is poured out on the desolate."

This antichrist (this end-of-time false christ or messiah) will set up his kingdom. He will call it the kingdom of God; however, it will definitely be a counterfeit kingdom. This is what 90% of the Book of Revelation is all about. It is a detailed account of what will happen during those seven years and specifically the last three and a half years known as the "Great Tribulation Period." It ends in a battle called "Armageddon," which never really happens, because of the return (Second Coming) of Jesus the King.

At the end of this seven year period of tribulation, Jesus will return as King and fulfill all the prophecies of the Bible concerning Him. He will return as the warrior King, not the suffering Messiah.

It says of Him (Jesus) at that time He will be covered with blood; however, this time it won't be His blood– it will be the blood of His enemies. Who are Jesus' enemies?

Jesus said in Matthew 12:29--
He who is not with Me is against Me.....
Everyone that is not with Jesus is against Him
Trust me; you want to be with Him and not against Him!

The Jews, a Fulfillment of Prophecy

The Jewish people themselves are a fulfilled prophecy. Do you realize that in the entire history of mankind, that no people or nation that has been disbanded and scattered over the entire earth, has ever remained a people and returned to their land and became a nation again?! Only the Jews have done this. Obviously, it was by the mighty hand of God.

The Jews were scattered by the Roman Empire from their land of Israel in A.D. 70, and their ancient homeland of Israel was taken from them. They were dispersed into the entire world, into every country.

As you might imagine, God has something to say about this in His Word.

God proclaims that towards the end of time or in the last days, God would gather His chosen people back into their land of Israel.

Ezekiel 36:24-31
For I will take you from among the nations, gather you out of all countries, and bring you into your own land.
Then I will sprinkle clean water on you, and you shall be clean; I will cleanse you from all your filthiness and from all your idols.
I will give you a new heart and put a new spirit within you; I will take the heart of stone out of your flesh and give you a heart of flesh.
I will put My Spirit within you and cause you to walk in My statutes, and you will keep My judgments and do them.
Then you shall dwell in the land that I gave to your fathers; you shall be My people, and I will be your God.
I will deliver you from all your uncleannesses. I will call for the grain and multiply it, and bring no famine upon you.

And I will multiply the fruit of your trees and the increase of your fields, so that you need never again bear the reproach of famine among the nations.
Then you will remember your evil ways and your deeds that were not good; and you will loathe yourselves in your own sight, for your iniquities and your abominations.

The Valley of Dry Bones, a Metaphor for Israel

Ezekiel 37:1-28
The hand of the LORD came upon me and brought me out in the Spirit of the LORD, and set me down in the midst of the valley; and it was full of bones.
Then He caused me to pass by them all around, and behold, there were very many in the open valley; and indeed they were very dry.
And He said to me, "Son of man, can these bones live?" So I answered, "O Lord GOD, You know."
Again He said to me, "Prophesy to these bones, and say to them, 'O dry bones, hear the word of the LORD!'
Thus says the Lord GOD to these bones: "Surely I will cause breath to enter into you, and you shall live.
I will put sinews on you and bring flesh upon you, cover you with skin and put breath in you; and you shall live. Then you shall know that I am the LORD."

So I prophesied as I was commanded; and as I prophesied, there was a noise, and suddenly a rattling; and the bones came together, bone to bone.
Indeed, as I looked, the sinews and the flesh came upon them, and the skin covered them over; but there was no breath in them.
Then He said to me, "Prophesy to the breath, prophesy, son of man, and say to the breath, 'Thus says the Lord GOD: "Come from the four winds, O breath, and breathe on these slain, that they may live."'
So I prophesied as He commanded me, and breath came into them, and they lived, and stood upon their feet, an exceedingly great army.
Then He said to me, **"Son of man, these bones are the whole house of Israel**.*"*

...and I will make them one nation in the land, on the mountains of Israel; and one king shall be king over them all; they shall no longer be two nations, nor shall they ever be divided into two kingdoms again.
They shall not defile themselves anymore with their idols, nor with their detestable things, nor with any of their transgressions; but I will deliver them from all their dwelling places in which they have sinned, and will cleanse them. ***Then they shall be My people, and I will be their God.***
David My servant shall be king over them, and they shall all have one shepherd; they shall also walk in My judgments and observe My statutes, and do them.
Then they shall dwell in the land that I have given to Jacob My servant, where your *fathers dwelt; and they shall dwell there,*

they, their children, and their children's children, forever; and My servant David shall be their prince forever.
Moreover I will make a covenant of peace with them, and it shall be an everlasting covenant with them; I will establish them and multiply them, and I will set My sanctuary in their midst forevermore.
My tabernacle also shall be with them; indeed I will be their God, and they shall be My people.
The nations also will know that I, the LORD, sanctify Israel, when My sanctuary is in their midst forevermore.

God has not given up on Israel, as some are saying and have been saying for centuries. God will deal directly with Israel in the last seven years of man's time upon this earth.

Chapter 5

Heaven: Fact or Fiction?

Is There Such a Place as Heaven?

It is a wonderful thought. A place where there is no illness, no pain, only joy continually. Is there a place where we don't have to put on airs or try to impress people? A place where people are known for who they are, not how they physically look or dress or what kind of house they live in or the kind of car they drive?

Is this a real place or just a place that man has dreamed up to help him cope with everyday life?

Is heaven just a myth? Is it just man's desperate hope for something that really doesn't exist? Unfortunately, this is the view of many millions of people. This is very sad.

Genesis 1:1
In the beginning God created the <u>heavens</u> and the earth.

The Bible teaches that there are three areas called heaven. The first heaven is the sky over the earth. The second heaven is the universe above-- the stars, galaxies, etc. The third heaven is the dwelling place of God. That may be in another dimension or dimensions. Scientists and mathematicians now believe it can be shown that there are more than three dimensions and many even believe that there are as many as ten dimensions!

At the time of Creation, God called the sky heaven.

Genesis 1:8
And God called the firmament Heaven. (1st heaven)

At that same time he called the universe heaven. (2nd heaven)

Genesis 1:16
Then God made two great lights: the greater light to rule the day, and the lesser light to rule the night. He made the stars also

There appears to be a place known as the third heaven. This seems to be the place where God dwells. Paul speaks about being taken up to God's dwelling place.

2 Corinthians 12:2-4
I know a man in Christ who fourteen years ago was caught up to ***the third heaven****. Whether it was in the body or out of the body* (dead or alive) *I do not know– God knows.*
And I know that this man– whether in the body or apart from the body I do not know, but God knows– was caught up to paradise. He heard inexpressible things, things that man is not permitted to tell.

Bodies for Earth and Bodies for Heaven

We could not go to heaven in these earthly bodies. These bodies were created for the environment of the earth. They are vehicles for our soul and spirit to dwell in while on the earth. A body is a temporary abode for the soul and spirit. The human spirit is eternal. Once it is created, it will exist someplace forever, for all eternity.

1 Corinthians 15:49-54
And as we have borne the image of the man of dust, we shall also bear the image of the heavenly Man.
Now this I say, brethren, that flesh and blood cannot inherit the kingdom of God; nor does corruption inherit incorruption.
Behold, I tell you a mystery: We shall not all sleep, but we shall all be changed–
a moment, in the twinkling of an eye, at the last trumpet. For the trumpet will sound, and the dead will be raised incorruptible, and we shall be changed.
*For this **corruptible must put on incorruption**, and this mortal must put on immortality.*
*So when this corruptible has put on incorruption, and **this mortal has put on immortality**, then shall be brought to pass the saying that is written: "Death is swallowed up in victory."*

So our spirit must leave this body that it has been riding around in, and be placed into a body that is suited for another environment, known as heaven.

The Bible says mankind is made for and suited to the environment of this earth. We are actually made up of the thirteen elements of the earth.

Genesis 3:19
By the sweat of your brow you will eat your food until you return to the ground, since from it you were taken; for dust you are and to dust you will return.

So, the body returns to the earth, and the spirit continues on somewhere else. This is the most universal commonality of the entire human race, from the beginning until today.

Heaven is a place outside the space/time continuum. It may be in another dimension. It may be out beyond the farthest galaxies. We really don't have any idea. Anything we say would be a guess on our part.

We do know that every person that has ever lived has one thing in common. When they are "alive" as we call it, they walk, talk, think, laugh, do good to others or do evil to others. They breathe, eat, drink, and do all things that are common to man. However, when they die and are lying on a table and you are standing over them looking down, they do nothing! They are gone! It becomes very obvious; this was only a vessel they occupied for their time on this planet. Their soul or spirit is gone. Therefore, who are they really? Are they the body or are they soul and spirit?

Genesis 2:6-7
the LORD God formed the man from ***the dust of the ground*** *and breathed into his nostrils the breath of life, and the man became a living being.*

Genesis 3:17-19
Cursed is the ground because of you; through painful toil you will eat of it all the days of your life. It will produce thorns and thistles for you, and you will eat the plants of the field. By the sweat of your brow you will eat your food until you return to the ground, since from it you were taken; ***for dust you are and to dust you will return****.*

Not many have actually seen heaven. However, there have been a few. Those men in the Scriptures that have seen heaven, or the throne of God, when they try to describe it, they cannot accurately give an account of what they have seen. Heaven is so fantastic; man has no real words to describe it. How do you explain that you've seen something for which there are no words to describe so that the other person can get an accurate picture? Would you say streets of gold, gates of pearl, is really what they saw? I personally don't think so; it's just the best they can do with the words that are available.

Explain Today's World to a Cowboy

Imagine that you have gone back in time to, say, 1850 and are trying to explain our modern world to those folks. Just try to explain television. What words could you use to describe it? If you use the words, tube, radio wave, transmitter, signal, picture, transistor, or TV studio, the person you are explaining this to would have absolutely no idea what you were talking about. See what I mean?

We do know, however, heaven is the place where God dwells. Now take a look around you. Look at the design, and creativity and versatility in the world. If God created a place like this for man to dwell in, how much more imaginative would His dwelling place be?

1 Corinthians 2:9
Eye has not seen, nor ear heard, Nor have entered into the heart of man The things which God has prepared for those who love Him.

This Scripture declares God has prepared something so fantastic that we humans cannot even, in our wildest dreams, imagine it.

New Heaven and a New Earth

Revelation 21:1-27
Now I saw a new heaven and a new earth, for the first heaven and the first earth had passed away. Also there was no more sea.
*Then I, John, saw the holy city, New Jerusalem, coming down out of Heaven from God, prepared as a bride adorned for her husband. And I heard a loud voice from heaven saying, "**Behold, the tabernacle of God is with men, and He will dwell with them, and they shall be His people. God Himself will be with***

them and be their God. [Restored the way it was in the Garden of Eden at the beginning.]

"And God will wipe away every tear from their eyes; there shall be no more death, nor sorrow, nor crying. There shall be no more pain, for the former things have passed away."

Then He who sat on the throne said, "Behold, I make all things new." And He said to me, "Write, for these words are true and faithful." And He said to me, "It is done! I am the Alpha and the Omega, the Beginning and the End. I will give of the fountain of the water of life freely to him who thirsts. "He who overcomes shall inherit all things, and I will be his God and he shall be My son. "But the cowardly, unbelieving, abominable, murderers, sexually immoral, sorcerers, idolaters, and all liars shall have their part in the lake which burns with fire and brimstone, which is the second death." Then one of the seven angels who had the seven bowls filled with the seven last plagues came to me and talked with me, saying, "Come, I will show you the bride, the Lamb's wife."

And he carried me away in the Spirit to a great and high mountain, and showed me the great city, the holy Jerusalem, descending out of heaven from God, having the glory of God. Her light was like a most precious stone, like a jasper stone, clear as crystal.

Also she had a great and high wall with twelve gates, and twelve angels at the gates, and names written on them, which are the names of the twelve tribes of the children of Israel:

three gates on the east, three gates on the north, three gates on the south, and three gates on the west. Now the wall of the city had twelve foundations, and on them were the names of the twelve apostles of the Lamb.

And he who talked with me had a gold reed to measure the city, its gates, and its wall. The city is laid out as a square; its length is as great as its breadth. And he measured the city with the reed: twelve thousand furlongs. Its length, breadth, and height are equal.

Then he measured its wall: one hundred and forty-four cubits, according to the measure of a man, that is, of an angel.

The construction of its wall was of jasper; and the city was pure gold, like clear glass. The foundations of the wall of the city were adorned with all kinds of precious stones: the first foundation was jasper, the second sapphire, the third chalcedony, the fourth emerald, the fifth sardonyx, the sixth sardius, the seventh chrysolite, the eighth beryl, the ninth topaz, the tenth chrysoprase, the eleventh jacinth, and the twelfth amethyst.

The twelve gates were twelve pearls: each individual gate was of one pearl. And the street of the city was pure gold, like transparent glass. But I saw no temple in it, for the Lord God Almighty and the Lamb are its temple. The city had no need of the sun or of the moon to shine in it, for the glory of God illuminated it. The Lamb is its light. And the nations of those who are saved shall walk in its light, and the kings of the earth bring their glory and honor into it.

Its gates shall not be shut at all by day (there shall be no night there). And they shall bring the glory and the honor of the nations into it. But there shall by no means enter it anything that defiles, or causes an abomination or a lie, but only those who are written in the Lamb's Book of Life.

Revelation 22:1-5

And he showed me a pure river of water of life, clear as crystal, proceeding from the throne of God and of the Lamb.
In the middle of its street, and on either side of the river, was the tree of life, which bore twelve fruits, each tree yielding its fruit every month. The leaves of the tree were for the healing of the nations. And there shall be no more curse, but the throne of God and of the Lamb shall be in it, and His servants shall serve Him. They shall see His face, and His name shall be on their foreheads.
There shall be no night there: They need no lamp nor light of the sun, for the Lord God gives them light. And they shall reign forever and ever.

This sounds like the place where one would certainly want to spend eternity, don't you think?

Chapter 6

The Fact of Hell

Hell is a very Misunderstood Place

There are two areas commonly referred to as hell. One of the areas referred to in the Bible and translated as hell or (Hades), is a place that is in the middle of the earth. This is not a permanent place; it is only a temporary holding area. The unrighteous dead will be held there until the "White Throne Judgment of God."

Prior to Christ's death and resurrection, Hades was split into two areas. One was called Paradise. It was also called Abraham's bosom, as this was the place of the righteous dead, the ones that were to be saved after the resurrection. The other side of Hades was the abode of the unsaved dead, the ones that were lost forever.

Righteous vs. Unrighteous

Let's quickly cover what constitutes righteousness and unrighteousness. The Bible states that the righteousness that God will receive is the righteousness of Jesus who was perfect, never committing a sin! You will, like the apostles, say, " Then whom will God receive into His kingdom?" For all mankind has sinned and fallen short of this definition of righteousness. The statement would be correct that no human being that has ever lived is without sin, with two exceptions: Adam before the Fall and Jesus.

Jesus, the Only Sinless Person who Ever Lived

2 Corinthians 5:21
*For he hath made him to be sin for us, **who knew no sin**; that we might be made the righteousness of God in him.*

Romans 6:23
For the wages of sin is death; but the gift of God is eternal life through Jesus Christ our Lord.

Ephesians 2:8-9
*For by grace are ye **saved through faith**; and that **not of yourselves**: it is the **gift of God**:*
***Not of works**, lest any man should boast.*

There is nothing you can do to be righteous before God, NOTHING! You are brought into the family of God through faith–period. You might ask, "Faith in what?" Faith in the fact that Jesus died and paid the price for your sin. The only catch is, you have to believe this.

When Jesus was being crucified, one of the thieves being crucified with Him, after admitting his crimes, said "Lord, remember me when **You come into Your kingdom**." Jesus said to him **"Today you will be with Me in Paradise,"** indicating where Jesus was going upon His physical death. This man did not have time to do good works, be baptized or to please God in any way. He was convicted, rightfully so, and was paying the price for the crimes he had committed. He simply believed in Jesus to save him and that belief **saved him**.

Matthew 12:40
For as Jonah was three days and three nights in the belly of the great fish, so will the Son of Man ***be three days and three nights*** *in* ***the heart of the earth***.

Jesus Empties Hell (Hades)

But after His resurrection, Jesus would lead all of those righteous dead from Paradise to heaven.

Ephesians 4:8-11
When He ascended on high, He led captivity captive, And gave gifts to men. Now this, "He ascended"–what does it mean but that He also first descended into the lower parts of the earth? He who descended is also the One who ascended far above all the heavens, that He might fill all things.

You might well ask, "What about the people that lived before Jesus come to earth? What about them? What about Abraham, Isaac, and Jacob?" As we mentioned before, hell or Hades is a place in the middle of the earth. However, it had two compartments, prior to Jesus' arrival on the earth. One part was called the abode of the unrighteous dead and the other was called Abraham's bosom or Paradise. Jesus tells the story of the Lazarus and the rich man in these places.

Jesus' Story about Hades (Hell)

Luke 16:19-31

There was a certain rich man who was clothed in purple and fine linen and fared sumptuously every day. But there was a certain beggar named Lazarus, full of sores, who was laid at his gate, desiring to be fed with the crumbs which fell from the rich man's table. Moreover the dogs came and licked his sores.
So it was that the beggar died, and was carried by the angels to Abraham's bosom. ***The rich man also died and was buried. And being in torments in Hades****, he lifted up his eyes and saw Abraham afar off, and Lazarus in his bosom. Then he cried and said, "Father Abraham, have mercy on me, and send Lazarus that he may dip the tip of his finger in water and cool my tongue; for I am tormented in this flame." But Abraham said, "Son, remember that in your lifetime you received your good things, and likewise Lazarus evil things; but now he is comforted and you are tormented. And besides all this, between us and you there is a great gulf fixed, so that those who want to pass from here to you cannot, nor can those from there pass to us." Then he said, "I beg you therefore, father, that you would send him to my father's house, for I have five brothers, that he may testify to them, lest they also come to this place of torment." Abraham said to him,* **"They have Moses and the prophets; let them hear them."** *[The Bible]* **And he said,** *"No, father Abraham; but if one goes to* ***them from the dead****, they will repent. But he said to*

him, ***"If they do not hear Moses and the prophets, neither will they be persuaded though one rise from the dead."***

Those that lived prior to Jesus' arrival on earth were saved by their faith that **God would send a savior**. That belief saved them. However, the Jews on the earth that rejected Jesus as their Messiah were in the lost category. This may sound intolerant, but that's what the Bible says, and I for one, believe it. One thing is for sure, the instant we die, at the exact moment of death, we will know for sure. Unfortunately for some, it will be too late!

Mankind Loves to Categorize Everything!

One is a Protestant; another is a Catholic, a Methodist, Hindu, Moslem, etc. However, this is not biblical. God in His Word has stated, there are just two groups of people on the earth. The first group is the saved. The second group is the lost.

The Real Hell's Permanent Location "Ghenennah"

Hell or Hades is only a temporary holding place. It is not permanent. Abraham's bosom was only a temporary holding place for the saved dead. No one could go to heaven or the dwelling place of God until the Messiah had come to do His redemptive work on earth.

There is however, a second place that is also referred to as hell in the Scriptures. It is called in Hebrew Ghenennah; it is also translated in our English Bibles as hell.

It is a permanent place. It was prepared for Satan and his fallen angels. It was never intended for man to go to this place. This is where the unsaved will be placed after the "White Throne Judgment" of God, at the end of time as we know it. The Bible says it will be a place of "outer darkness". There will be weeping and gnashing of teeth, a place of torment, a lake of fire, a place you do not want to go, under any circumstances.

The Great White Throne Judgment of God

Revelation 20:11-15
Then I saw a great white throne and Him who sat on it, from whose face the earth and the heaven fled away. And there was found no place for them.
And I saw the dead, small and great, standing before God*, and books were opened. And another book was opened, which is the* ***Book of Life****. And the dead were judged according to their works, by the things that were written in the books.*
The sea gave up the dead who were in it, and Death and ***Hades*** *delivered up the dead who were in them. And they were judged, each one according to his works.*
Then Death and Hades were cast into the lake of fire*.* [This is the second death.]
And anyone not found written in the Book of Life was cast into the lake of fire*.*

To end up in Ghenennah is called the second death. Physical death is the first death and separates your spirit or soul from your physical body. The second death is when your spirit is separated from God forever.

Remember God declares in the Bible there are but two groups of human beings, the lost and the saved. Think of that, every person who has ever lived is either lost for eternity or saved for eternity.

Hear and Respond

It couldn't be simpler. The Creator of all mankind has designed salvation in such a way, that you don't have to be an intellectual, and you don't even have to be smart. You just have to hear and respond. You have to be sincerely seeking God, your true Creator.

Unfortunately, the enemy of mankind, the devil called Satan with his evil realm, would like to confuse as many as possible about this subject. He would like you to believe that there is no heaven and no hell. If you don't believe in them, you are not going to worry about going to either and Satan has won! All cults and false religions have one major thing in common; They all teach that you have to work your way to God. There is something you have to do to please Him, to obtain salvation. The Bible teaches there is nothing you can do; Christ has done it all on the cross–you just have to believe and accept what Jesus has done for you by faith.

Lost or Saved for Eternity

Satan has been relatively successful over the years. The Bible does declare:

Matthew 7:13-14
Enter by the narrow gate; for ***wide is the gate*** *and broad is the way that leads to destruction, and there are* ***many*** *who go in by it.*
Because ***narrow is the gate*** *and difficult is the way which leads to life, and there* ***are few who find it****.*

We can see by this declaration that those who find the correct path are fewer than those who find the wrong way. That is a very scary thought. Just think about this statement for a moment. It is easier to go to hell than to heaven! Why is that? Because man's heart is inherently evil.

According to the Bible:

Romans 7:18
For I know that in me (that is, in my flesh) dwelleth no good thing:

Is Man Basically Good or Evil?

Jeremiah 17:9
The heart is deceitful above all things, and desperately wicked; who can know it?

To answer those critics who would say man is basically good, let's look at a little child. Did you ever notice that you don't have to teach a child to do bad things? He or she will do them naturally. He will learn to say "NO" as one of his first words. He will rebel without any lessons. He will steal without being taught. He will continually go downhill unless he is taught proper "good" behavior. Who ever taught a child to grab a toy and say "MINE"? You would never teach a child to say "mine." Then where does this come from? It comes from our humanness. It is part of our fallen nature. Man started out perfect and as he sinned and disobeyed God, he fell, and we (the human race) have been falling ever since, despite what the evolutionists tell us!

School Shootings

In the past years there has been a rash of school shootings in the United States. Everyone (the news media, and the government) has been trying to determine why, and to place blame. Of course, the number one enemy is those very bad guns, they say, as though an inanimate object can be either good or bad. It is the behavior of human beings that is either good or bad. Things can never be good or bad. If you place a loaded gun on the table, guess what? It will still be there a thousand years from now. It will probably be rusty, but it will never hurt anyone, ever, by itself.

I have heard when radio first was invented and gained popularity, there were those who said, "It is the tool of the devil!" In some cases, I'm sure that has a bit of truth in it. However, it has also been used as a tool for God, to enlighten many millions of people. Radio, like guns, is neither good nor bad. It is in the hands of people that it becomes either good or bad.

In the 1960s, in the wisdom of our intelligent leaders (the courts) we saw fit to remove prayer to our Creator from public schools. They also decided it was uncivilized to discipline students in the schools. It was considered child abuse. If you are a teacher, and you discipline a student, it is very likely that the student's parents will sue you.

In my school days, if you were to get into trouble at school, you would be dealt with harshly! However, that was not the thing that would most worry you. You would be most worried about your parents finding out about your school trouble. There would be hell to pay (as they say), when they found out. Thanks to the liberals in this society, that's all changed. Nowadays the parents take the side of their undisciplined, and often criminal, student and will readily sue the school, the principal and the poor teacher. No wonder some of our children are turning out the way they are. This ultimately teaches the student it is okay to be unrighteous, that bad and criminal behaviors are acceptable.

What is the reason for these schools shootings? It is so very simple! You remove moral teaching, prayer and discipline from the schools, and you will reap what you sow. It's not guns; it is a lack of discipline and moral teaching that are the total problem. In many cases, parents are too busy earning money to own a nicer house, newer car, etc. to properly raise their children. In many other cases the children **are just plain BAD**. No one in this society will ever say this. Some people, children included, are **JUST PLAIN BAD!** It doesn't have to be anyone else's fault. You can have two children raised in the same home, by the same parents, treated the same way; one becomes a pillar of the community, and the other is a serial killer. Why?

God has said over and over in His Word that man's heart is wicked. Who can know it? SOME PEOPLE ARE BAD – EVIL! Only God can change them, and believe me, they can change.

What is the enemy's plan? He will disrupt, cause chaos; he will do anything to keep mankind from finding the way of salvation, the correct path to God. As we witness in today's world, he is very good at what he does. He has deceived, and will continue to deceive, millions.

We have to recognize the enemy, the devil, for who and what he is, a destroyer of that which is good. He himself is lost, and his goal is to take as many human souls with him to hell as he can.

Saved from Hell

There are many promises in Scripture that those who are saved will not experience the second death with who will end up in hell.

There was the incident of Jesus' friend Lazarus. It seems that Lazarus had taken ill and died. Jesus had been healing the sick all around the upper Galilee area for some time, and Lazarus's sisters, Mary and Martha, sent for Jesus, because of all the strangers He had healed. Surely He would not hesitate to heal His good friend Lazarus? However, Jesus tarried; He delayed coming to Bethany. Upon arrival Martha was upset with Jesus, because Lazarus had been dead several days.

John 11:21-27
*Then Martha said to Jesus, "Lord, if You had been here, my brother would not have died." Jesus said to her, "Your brother will rise again." Martha said to Him, "I know that he will rise again in the resurrection at the last day." Jesus said to her, "**I am the resurrection and the life. He who believes in Me, though he may die, he shall live**. And whoever lives and believes in Me shall never die. Do you believe this?" She said to Him, "Yes, Lord, I believe that You are the Christ, the Son of God, who is to come into the world."*

At this point Jesus raised Lazarus from the dead!

John 14:1-6
*Let not your heart be troubled; you believe in God, believe also in me. In My Father's house are many mansions; if it were not so, I would have told you. I go to prepare a place for you. And if I go and prepare a place for you, I will come again and receive you to Myself; that where I am, there you may be also. And where I go you know, and the way you know. Thomas said to Him, "Lord, we do not know where You are going, and how can we know the way?" Jesus said to him, "I am the way, the truth, and the life. **No one comes to the Father except through Me."***

Jesus makes it clear that He has prepared a place for those who believe in Him. The Bible also makes it clear that there is a place for those who reject Him.

There is no middle ground; you are either for Jesus or against Him.

Chapter 7

The Fact of the Devil

Is Satan a Real Person?

The devil. He is an interesting character, to say the least. I would imagine 50% of the people in the United States do not believe he even exists. This is just what he wants. If you don't believe in him, you won't be watching out for his deception.

Satan makes his debut in the Bible:

Genesis 3:1-8
Now the serpent was more cunning than any beast of the field which the LORD God had made. And he said to the woman, "Has God indeed said, 'You shall not eat of every tree of the garden'?"
And the woman said to the serpent, "We may eat the fruit of the trees of the garden; but of the fruit of the tree which is in the midst of the garden, God has said, 'You shall not eat it, nor shall you touch it, lest you die.'" Then the serpent said to the woman, ***"You will not surely die****." "For God knows that in the day you eat of it your eyes will be opened,* ***<u>and you will be like God</u>****, knowing good and evil." So when the woman saw that the tree* ***was good for food****, that it was* ***pleasant to the eyes****, and a tree* ***desirable to make one wise****, she took of its fruit and ate. She also gave to her husband with her, and he ate. Then the eyes of*

both of them were opened, and they knew that they were naked; and they sewed fig leaves together and made themselves coverings.

Satan Calls God a Liar

Satan tells Eve that God is withholding something good from her. This is what he is still doing today.

Adam and Eve tried to cover their sin with something they could do (works, "fig leaves"). They sewed coverings for their bodies. It didn't work then and it doesn't work now. Man by himself cannot do works to cover his sin. God came down and killed animals (shedding of blood) to cover Adam and Eve, and temporarily fixed man's sin.

Who is Satan and where did he come from? Evidently, Lucifer, the name given to him at his creation, means "Son of the Morning."

The Bible tells us that he was created perfect and that he was a cherub, probably the cherub in charge of all the others. It appears he was number one in ranking right below God. (It might help to know that cherubs are not those cute little baby angels depicted in the paintings of the old masters, but rather powerful beings in God's service.)

Lucifer Originally Created Perfect

Ezekiel 28:13-19

You were the seal of perfection, Full of wisdom and perfect in beauty. You were in Eden, the garden of God; every precious stone was your covering: The sardius, topaz, and diamond, Beryl, onyx, and jasper, Sapphire, turquoise, and emerald with gold. The workmanship of your timbrels and pipes was prepared for you on the day you were created. You were the anointed cherub who covers [number one]; I established you; You were on the holy mountain of God; You walked back and forth in the midst of fiery stones. You were perfect in your ways from the day you were created, **till iniquity was found in you.**

By the abundance of your trading you became filled with violence within, and you sinned; therefore I cast you as a profane thing Out of the mountain of God; and I destroyed you, O covering cherub, from the midst of the fiery stones.

Your heart was lifted up **<u>because of your beauty</u>**; *You corrupted your wisdom for the sake of your splendor; I cast you to the ground, I laid you before kings, That they might gaze at you.*
You defiled your sanctuaries By the multitude of your iniquities, By the iniquity of your trading; Therefore I brought fire from your midst; It devoured you, And I turned you to ashes upon the earth In the sight of all who saw you. All who knew you among the peoples are astonished at you; You have become a horror, And shall be no more forever.

Satan's Fall

Isaiah 14:12-17

How you are fallen from heaven, O Lucifer, son of the morning! How you are cut down to the ground, You who weakened the nations! For you have said in your heart: ***I will*** *ascend into heaven,* ***I will*** *exalt my throne above the stars of God;* ***I will*** *also sit on the mount of the congregation On the farthest sides of the north;* ***I will*** *ascend above the heights of the clouds,* ***I will*** *be like the Most High.* ***Yet you shall be brought down to Sheol, To the lowest depths of the Pit****. Those who see you will gaze at you, And consider you, saying: "Is this the man who made the earth tremble, Who shook kingdoms,* ***Who made the world as a wilderness And destroyed its cities, Who did not open the house of his prisoners****?"*

Act of God

After reading this, you may think twice about calling tragedies "Acts of God."

"Act of God" – we have all heard this term and it's the wrong choice of words. The problems that this world has with everything: disasters, disease, death, and misery, can be directly attributed to Satan, demonic spirits and the rebellion of man himself. God doesn't rain misery on us; we do it well enough on our own.

Satan actually thought he was going to become God! There are false religions or cults today that teach the same thing. That by doing something (good works), man will ascend to become a god.

Isaiah 46:9-10
Remember the former things, those of long ago; ***I am God, and there is no other****;* ***I am God, and there is none like me****. I make known the* ***end from the beginning, from ancient times, what is still to come****[Prophecy].* *I say: My purpose will stand, and I will do all that I please.*

All of the trouble–disasters, disease, death, and misery–that has befallen man over the centuries can be traced to one event, the fall of Lucifer or Satan. If Satan hadn't fallen, he would not have tempted Eve.

When Jesus was on earth, during his three-year public ministry, He spent much of His time and effort dealing with Satan and demons. If this subject matter was so important that Jesus Himself spent a significant portion of His time dealing with it, what makes us think that this problem (Satan and demonic spirits) is not still a major problem in this world?

The Devil (Satan) is Single-minded

The Devil and his cohorts have only one goal: to deceive as many people as possible and take them as hostage to hell. It is not a good place.

Matthew 7:13-14

Enter by the narrow gate; for ***wide is the gate*** *and broad is the way that leads to destruction, and there are* ***many*** *who go in by it.*

Because ***narrow is the gate*** *and difficult is the way which leads to life, and there* ***are few who find it****.*

Chapter 8

Who is Jesus?

Famous

To start with, He is the most famous person who has ever lived on this earth. More has been written about Him than any other person in history. Millions of people have sacrificed their lives and have gone to their deaths for Him. We set our dates by His death!

He was not just a man with nice or good teachings! He was a man with a mission: to save mankind, who could not save themselves!

The Entire Bible is about One Person, Jesus

The whole entire Bible, Old Testament and New Testament, was written of Him.

Hebrews 10:7
Then I said, "Behold, I have come–
In the volume of the book it is written of Me–
To do Your will, O God."

John 5:38-39

You search the Scriptures, for in them you think you have eternal life; and these are they which testify of Me.

Understand that at the time of Jesus there was only what we call the "Old Testament." If the Old Testament was written about Him, and we know the New Testament is written about Him, then the entire Bible was written about Him.

All of the stories of the Bible are about the Messiah, whom God would send to save mankind, or the people of the Messiah. It is about how God called a certain man, and how that man became a people, and these people became a nation, and from this man and this people, came a savior, Jesus, just as God promised Adam in the Garden of Eden.

Genesis 3:15
And I will put enmity between you [Satan] *and the woman, and between your offspring and hers; he will crush your head, and you will strike his heel.*

There is only one thing you **can't say** about Jesus, and that is that he was just a "nice man with good teachings!" You might ask: "What do you mean by this statement?" He was either who He said He was–God come in the flesh, the one prophesied to save mankind–or He was deranged, and was the biggest deceiver who ever lived. He claimed to be the Son of God, and equal with God, and yet He continually taught us to obey the Scriptures and to not lie. How could He Himself lie? He did not, of course.

Jesus did not leave any middle ground for man. You either believe Him, or you don't. He said: "If you are not for Me, you are against Me."

Belief in Jesus will Divide Families

Matthew 10:35-36
For I have come to "set a man against his father, a daughter against her mother, and a daughter-in-law against her mother-in-law;" a man's enemies will be those of his own household.

What in the world did He mean by this statement? Believing in Him would divide households and families. We're back to those groups who are lost and those who are saved, but now it's even within our own families.

Jesus had the audacity to claim to be the only door to reconciliation with God through which we might obtain salvation.

John 10:7-9
Then Jesus said to them again, "Most assuredly, I say to you, I am the door of the sheep. All who ever came before Me are thieves and robbers, but the sheep did not hear them. ***I am the door. If anyone enters by Me, he will be saved****, and will go in and out and find pasture.*

Acts 4:10-12
Let it be known to you all, and to all the people of Israel, that by the name of Jesus Christ of Nazareth, whom you crucified,

whom God raised from the dead, by Him this man stands here before you whole. This is the stone that was rejected by you builders, which has become the chief cornerstone. ***Nor is there salvation in any other****, for there is* ***no other name under heaven given among men by which we must be saved****.*

Mohammed or Buddha or any other mere man cannot save you. You might ask, "What sets Jesus apart from all the others who came before Him and after Him?".

All the others are in their graves! Jesus' grave is empty! When Jesus rose from the earth into heaven, God was saying that this is the standard He will accept. So if you want to enter into heaven on your own, you will have to be perfect, never committing one sin, ever! You will have to be perfect, just as Jesus was, which means you won't get there on your own.

Every Christian who quotes these verses will hear in reply, "That's not fair; you have to accept Jesus to be saved?" The simple answer to this age-old question is **YES!**

God said the wages of sin is death! Death means separation of the spirit or soul from your physical body. The second death as stated in the Bible is the separation from God forever! God said in His Word: "Don't fear them that can kill your body, rather fear them that can steal your soul and condemn you to an eternity separated from God."

Matthew 10:28
And do not fear those who kill the body but cannot kill the soul. But rather fear Him who is able to destroy both soul and body in hell.

The Laws of God

When God set up His laws in Leviticus, He stated the rules and regulations which would tell man how he was going to relate to God since man's fall.

God said, "Without the shedding of blood there is no remission of sin." The Jews had to sacrifice innocent bulls and goats and through the continual shedding of blood there was forgiveness for a time. However, they had to continue to sacrifice over and over again to continue to cover their sins.

The Passover

When the Passover took place in Egypt, God said to His people, "Take a lamb without spot (perfect) and sacrifice it." "Take the blood of that lamb and wipe it on the lentil and door post and the Angel of Death will pass over that house." If they did not do this, the firstborn of each house would die. [***Note:*** anyone who did this, Jew or Egyptian (non-Jew), believing God, would be spared. The test was: did they believe God?]

In the New Testament, it is revealed that this Passover, as it is called, was a foreshadowing of the very act that would satisfy

God and would reconcile God and man together again forever and for all time and eternity.

Jesus was killed on the same day of the year as the lamb had been killed; His blood was shed on Passover. Can you see the significance?

When John the Baptist first saw Jesus coming to him to be baptized, he made the following statement:

The Lamb of God

John 1:29
The next day John saw Jesus coming toward him, and said, "Behold! ***The Lamb of God who takes away the sin of the world!"***

John called Him a Lamb.

This was the ultimate sacrifice; God's only begotten Son died on a cross that was meant for us. He suffered the death that we deserve, so that we would never have to know or experience separation from God as He did on the cross.

A Creator's Love

Those of you with children, for what cause would you sacrifice your only son or child? You would have to love someone or something a great deal to make such a sacrifice.

This was no small thing that was done by Jesus. He was God, the Creator of the universe: "All things were created by and for Him." And yet He loved us so much that He gave up what He had before, permanently for all time and eternity. He did not go back to being in the form what He was before; He is still very much Almighty God, but I believe He became different in form, and He became what we will be. The Bible says that for the ages to come we will continually know how much he loved us. How? Because we will see Him as a lamb that was slain, for us!

Who is Jesus really?

As we have previously read, the entire Bible, Old Testament and New Testament, is written of Him.

The Bible teaches there is one God. It states that this one God is manifested in three distinct persons. This is a concept that our human brains have a hard time understanding. Let me see if I can put it into easier terms.

One God, Three Persons

The one God is one being, and within this one being there are three persons. You and I are human beings. We are all human beings; however, within beings called humans there are billions of us. Within the being called God, there are just three. They are called the Father, Son and Holy Spirit.

In the Book of Colossians, Paul the Apostle speaks of Jesus:

Colossians 1:13-18

He has delivered us from the power of darkness and conveyed us into the kingdom of the Son of His love, in whom we have redemption through His blood, the forgiveness of sins. He is the image of the invisible God, the firstborn over all creation. ***For by Him (Jesus) all things were created that are in heaven and that are on earth, visible and invisible, whether thrones or dominions or principalities or powers. All things were created through Him (Jesus) and for Him (Jesus). And He is before all things, and in Him (Jesus) all things consist****. And He is the head of the body, the church, who is the beginning, the firstborn from the dead, that in all things He may have the preeminence.*

All things were created by Him and for Him, what a statement! In Him all things consist. That means He is holding all things together by His power. This statement is either true or false!

Scientists don't understand what holds neutrons and protons spinning within an atom together, for their natural tendency is to repel each other.

Scientists have come up with ideas like atomic glue! The Bible says Jesus is holding this entire universe together. Jesus is the Creator!

Let's get back to what is called the Trinity: Father, Son and Holy Spirit. When man was created, he was created with body, soul and spirit. In this life we judge each other by the looks of our bodies. However, this is not the real you! You are really soul and spirit and are merely riding around in this body that is adapted for this particular world. When I was young, I had an aunt. I knew her only as an old, old lady. One day I saw a picture of her when she was young. I thought to myself: she was beautiful. If we live long enough, all of us completely lose all of our earthly beauty.

Communing with God Face to Face

In the Garden of Eden, God communed with man face-to-face. God is Father, Son and Spirit. Man is body, soul and spirit. Which attribute is common between man and God? You are correct if you said, "Spirit."

When man disobeyed God in the garden, his spirit died. He had no way to commune with God face-to-face any longer.

Genesis 2:17
but of the tree of the knowledge of good and evil you shall not eat, for in the day that you eat of it ***you shall surely die****.*

They did not die physically that day; however, they did die spiritually, which was worse. They eventually died physically also. God in His mercy would not let man continue living in his sinful body forever. After a number of years, He would release him.

Born Again

Why is this spiritual death concept so important? Jesus had a conversation with a Pharisee named Nicodemus who asked this question of Jesus:

John 3:1-8
There was a man of the Pharisees named Nicodemus, a ruler of the Jews. This man came to Jesus by night and said to Him, "Rabbi, we know that You are a teacher come from God; for no one can do these signs that You do unless God is with him." Jesus answered and said to him, "Most assuredly, I say to you, unless one is ***born again****, he cannot see the kingdom of God." Nicodemus said to Him, "How can a man be born when he is old? Can he enter a second time into his mother's womb and be born?" Jesus answered, "Most assuredly, I say to you, unless one is born of water and the Spirit, he cannot enter the kingdom of God. That which is born of the flesh is flesh, and that* ***which is born of the Spirit is spirit.*** *Do not marvel that I said to you,* ***'You must be born again****.' "*

Jesus is saying your spirit must be "born again." Your dead **spirit must be made alive again before you physically die** in order to enter into the kingdom of heaven.

This then is the key to salvation. You must be born again. This term has been tossed around by the media and ridiculed; however, it is the key to salvation.

How is your spirit born again?

Acts 4:10-12
Let it be known to you all, and to all the people of Israel, that ***by the name of Jesus Christ*** *of Nazareth, whom you crucified, whom God raised from the dead, by Him this man stands here*

before you whole. This is the stone that was rejected by you builders, which has become the chief cornerstone. ***Nor is there salvation in any other****, for there is* ***no other name under heaven*** *given among men by which we must be saved.*

What then is salvation? Salvation is being saved! Saved from what? Saved from the condemnation that mankind has brought upon himself, an eternal separation from God, going to a "place of unending horror and pain." Therefore, salvation is being saved from this horrible place and getting to live with God in a glorious place, heaven. It's really pretty simple.

Restored to God

We are going to be restored to God and restored to being the way God intended us to be back in the Garden of Eden.

You have to have an understanding of these things to be able to understand Jesus' mission, and why He came to the earth.

As mentioned before, man turned over the "Title Deed" of the earth to Satan. Guess what? He still has it, but not for long!

Jesus, by His sacrificial death on the cross has purchased us back to God. He paid the price for sin on our behalf and experienced separation from the Father, so we would not have to experience that separation.

God is longsuffering, and not willing that any should perish, but that all would come to repentance, and accept His Son's sacrificial death that pays the debt and redeems mankind and the earth back to God.

Romans 8:18-22

For I consider that the sufferings of this present time are not worthy to be compared with the glory which shall be revealed in us. For the earnest expectation of the creation eagerly waits for the revealing of the sons of God. For the creation was subjected to futility, not willingly, but because of Him who subjected it in hope; because the creation itself also will be delivered from the bondage of corruption into the glorious liberty of the children of God.

For we know that the whole creation groans and labors with birth pangs together until now.

The Catch to Salvation

God has made reconciliation with mankind through the obedience of this Son Jesus and His great sacrifice.

There is only one catch! You have to acknowledge what God, through Jesus, did on your behalf. Did you know even in our modern-day *jurisprudence* that if you are sentenced to death and the convening authority–let's say the governor–gives you a full pardon, you can walk away free? However, if you don't accept the pardon, you will certainly be put to death, even though you have been pardoned.

So it is with redemption. God, through His Son Jesus, has paid the price and given you a pardon. The only thing you have to do is accept it to make it valid.

Why in the world would an individual not accept such a gift? Let's review: The title deed to the earth is still in the hands of the evil one, Satan. He has as his main goal to stop you from making this decision. He wants to take as many souls to eternal damnation as he possibly can. His forte is deception!

The Bible says that Satan is a liar and the father of lies. He is a master deceiver. He will deceive through the good works of a false religion, or through involving one in any number of sins. He will do anything to keep you from the truth. Trust me when I say, that he is extremely intelligent and thousands of times smarter than the smartest human being. He understands all languages and all the laws of physics and science. I'm sure he is a master of them all. I'm sure he looks at us as being another animal. It probably annoys him that God has lavished so much love on us. He doesn't get it, because his heart is evil.

One false religion even dares to declare Satan as a blood brother of Jesus. They claim that Satan really wanted to save mankind, but that task was given to Jesus instead. Who authored this religious cult? I'll give you one guess!

So that you understand perfectly, Jesus is definitely God. He is the Son, the Second Person of the triune Godhead. Satan, on the other hand is a created being, created by God the Son. They are not equal in any way, although this is the stated goal of Satan.

Isaiah 14:13-14

For thou hast said in thine heart, I will ascend into heaven, I will exalt my throne above the stars of God: I will sit also upon the mount of the congregation, in the sides of the north: I will ascend above the heights of the clouds; I will be like the most High.

Satan is not satisfied being a cherub; he wants to be God or like God. It will never happen.

Isaiah 44:6

Thus saith the LORD the King of Israel, and his redeemer the LORD of hosts; I am the first, and I am the last; ***and beside me there is no God.***

He is the one and only God; there has never been and will never be another God.

John 3:17-18

For God sent not his Son into the world ***to condemn the world****; but that the* ***world through him might be saved****. He that believeth on him is not condemned****: but he that believeth not is condemned already****, because he hath not believed in the name of the only begotten Son of God.*

As the Scripture says in John 3:17 and 18, we are already condemned; we are condemned waiting for a savior. That savior came 2000 years ago. His own people rejected Him, fulfilling Bible prophecy.

Matthew 27:22-25
Pilate saith unto them, What shall I do then with Jesus which is called Christ? They all say unto him, ***Let him be crucified****. And the governor said, Why, what evil hath he done? But they cried out the more, saying, Let him be crucified. When Pilate saw that he could prevail nothing, but that rather a tumult was made, he took water, and washed his hands before the multitude, saying, I am innocent of the blood of this just person: see ye to it.* ***Then answered all the people, and said, His blood be on us, and on our children.***

This was an enormously bad thing to declare. The Jews not only took the responsibility and the blame on themselves, but also on all future generations of Jews. Out of their own lips they condemned themselves.

Just before Jesus made His triumphal entry into Jerusalem in A.D. 32, He stopped on the crest of the Mount of Olives and said:

Luke 13:34-35
O Jerusalem, Jerusalem, the one who kills the prophets and stones those who are sent to her! How often I wanted to gather your children together, as a hen gathers her brood under her wings, ***but you were not willing!*** *See! Your house is left to you* ***desolate****; and assuredly, I say to you, you shall not see Me until the time comes when you say,* ***"Blessed is He who comes in the name of the Lord!"***

Basically, Jesus held them accountable to know prophecy. The very day was foretold by the prophet Daniel, but they did not recognize it when it occurred. Instead they rejected Him, as do all of us, prior to knowing Him.

Chapter 9

How to Get to Heaven

Get on the Right Road to Eternity

God in His wisdom has made it as easy as possible to be saved, to have your sins forgiven. You do not have to be a great scholar or an intellectual or even very smart to find the correct path. You do have to have a **sincere desire** to know the **One True God** and **His plan for your life**. If you are sincerely seeking God, He will reveal Himself to you.

Jesus said: "All others are thieves and robbers." Why did He say this? There will be many who will come claiming to be the Messiah/Savior.

Here are a few of the promises from the Word of God concerning your salvation. Remember, it is easy to take Scriptures out of context, so open a Bible and do your homework; study these passages in their proper context.

John 10:7-18
Then Jesus said to them again, *"Most assuredly, I say to you, I am the door of the sheep. All who ever came before Me are thieves and robbers, but the sheep did not hear them. I am the door. If anyone enters by Me,* ***he will be saved****, and will go in and out and find pasture."*

John 3:19

And this is the condemnation, that the light has come into the world, and men ***loved darkness rather than light****, because their* ***deeds were evil****.*

John 3:16

For God so loved the world that He gave His only begotten Son, that whoever believes in Him should not perish but have everlasting life.

John 3:17-18

For God did not send His Son into the world to condemn the world, but that the world ***through Him might be saved****.*

He who believes in Him is not condemned; but he who does not believe ***is condemned already****, because he has not believed in the name of* ***the only begotten Son of God****.*

John 10:10-18

The thief does not come except to steal, and to kill, and to destroy. I have come that they may have life, and that they may have it more abundantly. I am the good shepherd. ***The good shepherd gives His life for the sheep****. But a hireling, he who is not the shepherd, one who does not own the sheep, sees the wolf coming and leaves the sheep and flees; and the wolf catches the sheep and scatters them. The hireling flees because he is a hireling and does not care about the sheep. I am the good shepherd; and I know My sheep, and am known by My own. As the Father knows Me, even so I know the Father;* ***and I lay down My life for the sheep****.*

And other sheep I have which are not of this fold; them also I must bring, and ***they will hear My voice****; and there will be* ***one flock and one shepherd.*** *Therefore My Father loves Me, because I lay down My life that I may take it again. No one takes it from Me, but I lay it down of Myself.* ***I have power to lay it down, and I have power to take it again****. This command I have received from My Father.*

Acts 2:21

And it shall come to pass that <u>whoever</u> ***calls on the name of the Lord shall be <u>saved.</u>***

Acts 4:11-12

Nor is there salvation in any other*, for there is* ***no other name under heaven given among men by which we must be saved.***

Acts 16:30-31

*And he brought them out and said, "Sirs, what must I do to be saved?" So they said, "****Believe on the Lord Jesus Christ, and you will be saved****, you and your household."*

Romans 10:9

If you ***confess with your mouth*** *the Lord Jesus and* ***believe in your heart*** *that God has raised Him from the dead****, you will be saved****.*

Ephesians 2:8-10

For by grace you have been saved through faith, and that not of yourselves; ***it is the gift of God, <u>not of works</u>****, lest anyone should boast. For we are His workmanship, created in Christ*

Jesus for good works, which God prepared beforehand that we should walk in them.

1 Timothy 2:3-5
For there is one God and one Mediator between God and men, the Man Christ Jesus,

2 Timothy 1:9-10
who has saved us and called us with a holy calling, ***not according to <u>our works</u>****, but according to His own purpose and* ***<u>grace</u>*** *which was given to us in* ***Christ Jesus before time began****, but has now been revealed by the appearing of our* ***Savior Jesus Christ****, who has abolished death and brought life and immortality to light* ***through the gospel.***

The foregoing are but a few Scriptures indicating that we must be saved to enter into the kingdom of God. If we are not saved, then we are lost. Lost to God forever, an eternity without God, without anything good or right.

Follow the Bereans' Example

Please don't take my word for these truths. Paul, in the Book of Acts, states that the Berean people were more noble, because they learned of these truths; but they did not take Paul's word for it. It
states that they searched the Scriptures daily to make sure Paul was telling the truth.

Acts 17:11
Now the Bereans were of more noble character than the Thessalonians, for they received the message with great eagerness and examined the Scriptures every day to see if what Paul said was true.

That's just what you should do. Don't take any man's word for the truths of the Scriptures. Check them out for yourself. Put the time and study in so you can be assured of your eternal home.

This is not a difficult task. Remember, if you are not sincerely seeking the truth, you will not find it.

1 Corinthians 2:14
*But the natural man does not receive the things of the Spirit of God, for they are foolishness to him; nor can he know them, because they are **spiritually discerned**.*

Spiritual Discernment

Things of the spirit are "spiritually discerned." God reveals the truths of His Word to those who are sincerely seeking God and wanting to know God's truths.

The entire Bible is speaking of Jesus, because He is the only way to God. Some may say that is not politically correct, but it is the truth! Jesus didn't come to earth under the best of circumstances. However, He led a **perfect life (Jesus**

personally never committed a single sin), which was acceptable to God. When we accept Him (Jesus) as our personal Savior, His righteousness is substituted for our unrighteousness, and we become righteous in the eyes of God, because Jesus bore our sins on the cross and became our substitute.

Upon Jesus' departure from the apostles, he gave them a promise.

John 14:2-6
In My Father's house are many mansions; if it were not so, I would have told you. I go to prepare a place for you. And if I go and prepare a place for you, ***I will come again and receive you to Myself; that where I am, there you may be also.*** *And where I go you know, and the way you know. Thomas said to Him, "Lord, we do not know where You are going, and how can we know the way?" Jesus said to him, "I am the way, the truth, and the life.* ***No one comes to the Father except through Me."***

When we make this decision, what do we have to look forward to? Like all good books, the answer is in the back of the book.

New Heaven and a New Earth

Remember the word *revelation* means to revel that which was previously unknown.

Revelation 21

Now I saw a new heaven and a new earth, for the first heaven and the first earth had passed away. Also there was no more sea.

Then I, John, saw the holy city, New Jerusalem, coming down out of heaven from God, prepared as a bride adorned for her husband.

And I heard a loud voice from heaven saying, ***"Behold, the tabernacle of God is with men, and He will dwell with them, and they shall be His people. God Himself will be with them and be their God.***

"And God will wipe away every tear from their eyes; there shall be no more death, nor sorrow, nor crying. There shall be no more pain, for the former things have passed away."

Then He who sat on the throne said, ***"Behold, I make all things new****." And He said to me, "Write, for* ***these words are true and faithful****."*

And He said to me, "It is done! I am the Alpha and the Omega, the Beginning and the End. I will give of the fountain of the water of life freely to him who thirsts.

"He who overcomes shall inherit all things, and I will be his God and he shall be My son.

"But the cowardly, unbelieving, abominable, murderers, sexually immoral, sorcerers, idolaters, and all liars shall have their part in the lake which burns with fire and brimstone, which is the second death."

Then one of the seven angels who had the seven bowls filled with the seven last plagues came to me and talked with me, saying, "Come, I will show you the bride, the Lamb's wife."

And he carried me away in the Spirit to a great and high mountain, and showed me the great city, the holy Jerusalem, descending out of heaven from God,
having the glory of God. Her light was like a most precious stone, like a jasper stone, clear as crystal.
Also she had a great and high wall with twelve gates, and twelve angels at the gates, and names written on them, which are the names of the twelve tribes of the children of Israel:
three gates on the east, three gates on the north, three gates on the south, and three gates on the west.
Now the wall of the city had twelve foundations, and on them were the names of the twelve apostles of the Lamb.
And he who talked with me had a gold reed to measure the city, its gates, and its wall.
The city is laid out as a square; its length is as great as its breadth. And he measured the city with the reed: twelve thousand furlongs. Its length, breadth, and height are equal.
Then he measured its wall: one hundred and forty-four cubits, according to the measure of a man, that is, of an angel.
The construction of its wall was of jasper; and the city was pure gold, like clear glass.
The foundations of the wall of the city were adorned with all kinds of precious stones: the first foundation was jasper, the second sapphire, the third chalcedony, the fourth emerald,
the fifth sardonyx, the sixth sardius, the seventh chrysolite, the eighth beryl, the ninth topaz, the tenth chrysoprase, the eleventh jacinth, and the twelfth amethyst.
The twelve gates were twelve pearls: each individual gate was of one pearl. And the street of the city was pure gold, like transparent glass.

But I saw no temple in it, for the Lord God Almighty and the Lamb are its temple.
The city had no need of the sun or of the moon to shine in it, for the glory of God illuminated it. The Lamb is its light.
And the nations of those who are saved shall walk in its light, and the kings of the earth bring their glory and honor into it.
Its gates shall not be shut at all by day (there shall be no night there).
And they shall bring the glory and the honor of the nations into it.
But there shall by no means enter it anything that defiles, or causes an abomination or a lie, but only those who are written in the Lamb's Book of Life.

Revelation 22
And he showed me a pure river of water of life, clear as crystal, proceeding from the throne of God and of the Lamb.
In the middle of its street, and on either side of the river, was the tree of life, which bore twelve fruits, each tree yielding its fruit every month. The leaves of the tree were for the healing of the nations.
And there shall be no more curse, but the throne of God and of the Lamb shall be in it, and His servants shall serve Him.
They shall see His face, and His name shall be on their foreheads.
There shall be no night there: They need no lamp nor light of the sun, for the Lord God gives them light. And they shall reign forever and ever.

Then he said to me, "These words are faithful and true." And the Lord God of the holy prophets sent His angel to show His servants the things which must shortly take place.

"Behold, I am coming quickly! Blessed is he who keeps the words of the prophecy of this book."

Now I, John, saw and heard these things. And when I heard and saw, I fell down to worship before the feet of the angel who showed me these things.

Then he said to me, "See that you do not do that. For I am your fellow servant, and of your brethren the prophets, and of those who keep the words of this book. Worship God."

And he said to me, "Do not seal the words of the prophecy of this book, for the time is at hand.

"He who is unjust, let him be unjust still; he who is filthy, let him be filthy still; he who is righteous, let him be righteous still; he who is holy, let him be holy still."

"And behold, I am coming quickly, and My reward is with Me, to give to every one according to his work.

"I am the Alpha and the Omega, the Beginning and the End, the First and the Last."

Blessed are those who do His commandments, that they may have the right to the tree of life, and may enter through the gates into the city.

But outside are dogs and sorcerers and sexually immoral and murderers and idolaters, and whoever loves and practices a lie.

"I, Jesus, have sent My angel to testify to you these things in the churches. I am the Root and the Offspring of David, the Bright and Morning Star."

And the Spirit and the bride say, "Come!" And let him who hears say, "Come!" And let him who thirsts come. Whoever desires, let him take the water of life freely.
For I testify to everyone who hears the words of the prophecy of this book: If anyone adds to these things, God will add to him the plagues that are written in this book;
and if anyone takes away from the words of the book of this prophecy, God shall take away his part from the Book of Life, from the holy city, and from the things which are written in this book.
He who testifies to these things says, "Surely I am coming quickly." Amen. Even so, come, Lord Jesus!
The grace of our Lord Jesus Christ be with you all. Amen.

How to Get to Heaven the Easy Way

In summary, it is easy to go to heaven! The Bible, the Word of God, makes it clear that it is easy. You have only to believe. You don't have to understand all things, or be an intellectual, but you do have to have a sincere desire to know God and His plan for your life.

You will spend eternity somewhere. It's up to you where: heaven or hell! Remember, it's harder to believe the promises of God if you don't know God or His character. The Bible is the story of God and His love for mankind. The better you know the story, the easier it is to believe what God has promised those who love and obey Him.

At the very minimum, man should be willing to put in the time to make an informed decision that will determine where his soul will spend all of eternity. Wouldn't you agree?

A good place to start is what is called the sinner's prayer.

Acknowledge you are a sinner deserving of death and hell. Repent, which simply means to turn and go in the other direction. In other words, leave darkness in favor of the light. Ask God to forgive your sins and to come into your life and guide you on His path.

Just say this simple prayer:

"Dear God, Creator of heaven and earth and all that is in them, I acknowledge my sin and ask You to forgive me and help me to turn away from these sins and to follow You. Thank You that Your Son Jesus died on the cross and rose from the dead to pay the price for my sin. My desire is to walk with You all the days of my life and to spend eternity in heaven with You. I ask all of this in the name of Jesus the Christ. Amen."

If you said this prayer and sincerely meant it, you have been born again. It's just that easy. You are going to heaven the easy way!

Now begins a walk that will last the rest of your life. It will not always be easy; you now have an archenemy, Satan. He will do everything he possibly can to mess up your relationship with God. You're now in God's army. You will have to prepare yourself for the battles to come. You may lose a few; however, you have already won the war, and no one can take that away from you. You are saved and cannot be lost ever again.

Ephesians 6:11-17
Put on the whole armor of God, that you may be able to stand against the wiles of the devil. For we do not wrestle against flesh and blood, but against principalities, against powers, against the rulers of the darkness of this age, against spiritual hosts of wickedness in the heavenly places. Therefore take up the whole armor of God, that you may be able to withstand in the evil day, and having done all, to stand.
*Stand therefore, having girded your waist with **truth**, having put on the breastplate **of righteousness**, and having shod your feet with the preparation of the **gospel** of peace;*
*above all, taking the shield of **faith** with which you will be able to quench all the fiery darts of the wicked one. And take the helmet of **salvation**, and the sword of the **Spiri**t, which is the **word of God**;*

Jesus has promised that once you become a child of God, that not only is His hand around you, but the Father's hand is also around you, and no one can snatch you from Their safekeeping. What a comfort that is.

The next step is to find a good fellowship of believers. Being with other believers will help you in your walk and ultimately bring you into a better understanding of God.

Pick a church body that is devoted to teaching the Word of God. Above all, pray that God would lead you to a church body that will allow you to learn and know the true character of God and what His plan is for your life.

May God grant you wisdom in your lifelong quest to know your Heavenly Father and to establish an intimate relationship with Him.

John 10:28
And I give them eternal life, and they shall never perish; neither shall anyone snatch them out of ***My hand****.*

John 10:29-30
My Father, who has given them to Me, is greater than all; and no one is able to snatch them out of ***My Father's hand****.*

My prayer for you is that God grant you the wisdom and the power to make the right decision that will guarantee you a place in God's kingdom for all eternity.

The beginning of a new life with God

How to Get to Heaven – The Easy Way
40991 Highway 228
Sweet Home, OR 97386
Fax 541-367-4549

www.HowToGetToHeaven.org

Other valuable resources.

The Word For Today
P.O. Box 8000, Costa Mesa, CA 92628 1-800-272-WORD
www.TheWordForToday.org

Koinonia House Inc.
P.O. Box D, Coeur d'Alene, ID 83816 800-546-8731
www.khouse.org

Institute for Creation Research or ICR
P.O. Box 2667, El Cajon CA 92021
www.icr.org

Josh McDowell Ministry
PO Box 131000 · Dallas, Texas 75313· 972-907-1000
www.josh.org